I0657287

William Andrews

Curious church gleanings

William Andrews

Curious church gleanings

ISBN/EAN: 9783337161729

Printed in Europe, USA, Canada, Australia, Japan

Cover: Foto ©Lupo / pixelio.de

More available books at **www.hansebooks.com**

Curious Church Gleanings.

HULL:
WILLIAM ANDREWS & CO., THE HULL PRESS.
LONDON:
SIMPKIN, MARSHALL, HAMILTON, KENT & CO., LTD.

1896.

Preface.

THE welcome given by the public and the press to my previous volume issued under the title of " Curious Church Customs," has encouraged me to prepare on similar lines another collection of papers dealing with the byways and highways of Church history.

My contributors have done their best to furnish articles of interest, and I think their work is of permanent value. I should be ungrateful if I did not express my gratitude for their assistance.

I send forth this book hoping that it may not fail to prove entertaining, and throw some light on matters of interest to lovers of our National Church.

WILLIAM ANDREWS.

THE HULL PRESS,

St. Nicholas' Day, 1895.

Contents.

CURIOUS CHURCH GLEANINGS.

What to look for in an Old Church.

By George Benson.

THE church in many villages is the only object of antiquity. In it, generation after generation of the villagers have been baptised, married, and buried; on it, the best work of the village mason, joiner, smith, and carver has been employed, and a good deal of the village history is contained within its walls, rendering the edifice so interesting that even strangers rarely leave the village without a peep at the church. To render the visit to a village church as interesting as possible, we purpose explaining the various objects as we may meet them.

The church, with its burial ground, is enclosed by a wall.

1

> Each in its little plot of holy ground,
> How beautiful they stand,
> These old grey churches of our native land.

At the entrance to the churchyard is the lych-gate, or corpse gate (A.S., lich, a dead body), being a covered gateway, beneath which the coffin rests on a bier for a few minutes. Through the lychgate are the stocks, in which those who had been guilty of some minor offence were placed. Nearer the church is the tall churchyard cross, elaborately carved and raised on steps, from which in some places sermons are preached in fine weather. Scattered over the burial ground are yew trees, which, having a long life, are typical of immortality. At Easter, Whitsun-tide, and Christmas, boughs of this tree were used to decorate the interior of the church. The church-yard is filled with headstones, table tombs, etc., many of them inscribed with quaint and curious epitaphs.

The church, generally approached on the south side, consists of a tower at the west end; south porch and aisles, with roof sloping from below the windows of nave; and chancel, with priest's door. On the east end of the nave roof is a Sanctus bell cot, containing the bell which

was rung at the words "Sancte, sancte, sancte,
Deus Sabaoth" (Holy, holy, holy, Lord God of
Sabaoth); and all who heard it were expected
to prostrate themselves. The east end of the
chancel roof is terminated by a gable cross, richly
sculptured, and on the wall is a consecration
cross sculptured where the bishop when con-
secrating the church had made the sign of the
cross. The projecting pieces of masonry to the
wall are termed buttresses, and on some there are
deep furrows worn by sharpening arrows, when
archery was practised in the churchyard. The
buttresses terminate in gargoyles, projecting
grotesque figures, with open mouths, which carry
the water from the roof and throw it off the
building. On one side of the entrance to the
south porch is an ancient sun-dial, whilst above
the moulded arch is a canopied niche, containing
an effigy of the patron saint. Above is a window
which lights the room over the porch. Within
the porch on either side runs a stone bench, and
on the walls are posted the church notices. The
deeply moulded and shafted doorway is fitted with
a door made from the oak of Old England, and
enriched with beautiful bands of wrought ironwork
representing the Fall of Man.

Within the church, at the east side of the door, is a stone basin formed in the masonry. This is the "Stoup" used in mediæval days for holy water. On entering, each worshipper dipped his finger into it, and crossed himself. Sometimes a stoup is met with outside the priest's door. Opposite the entrance stands the font, of stone, lined with lead, and filled with water for baptism. It is deep and circular in shape, ornamented on the exterior, and surmounted with a lofty crocketed spire, raised by a pulley and a counterpoise in the form of a dove, so that as it ascends the holy dove descends. The font stands between the north and south doors. Through the former Satan is said to escape from the child when, by baptism, it becomes a child of Christ. Over the tower arch are the Royal Arms, and along the walls under the tower are tables recording the names of past benefactors to the poor, the parish, and the church. A bread board in the form of a carved cabinet with shelves, displays the loaves given to the poor who attend service in accordance with the wish of the benefactor.

Unlocking a door in the angle, the tower is ascended in corkscrew fashion by narrow, dusty, and ill-lighted stairs. Plodding up the decayed, broken, and rugged steps, a faint glimmering of light illuminates the darkness, gradually increasing until a low door is reached : stooping beneath, a large, lofty, and gloomy apartment is entered. This is the Ringing Chamber. A loud, sharp, metallic creaking noise arrests attention, and the clock apparatus is observed in the dim light. The great clock is about to strike, and for some minutes is preparing itself for the alarming event. Dangling from the ceiling are the ropes from the belfry ; on the floor is a carved oak settee for the ringers, and a highly ornamented chest full of disused rate books, with the banner of St. George and the Union Jack thrown carelessly over, and sometimes as carelessly hoisted on the staff, for we have noticed church flags gaily floating in the breeze upside down. From the windows of this chamber many charming views are obtained. Affixed to the walls are peal boards, recording achievements of former ringers, and also rules in rhyme relating to ringing, as follows :—

> He that a bell doth overthrow
> Shall twopence pay before he go,
> And he that rings with spur or hat
> Shall fourpence pay, be sure of that :
> And if these orders he refuse
> No less than sixpence will excuse.

By a dilapidated ladder in the corner the ascent is made to the belfry ; then passing through the trap door, the breeze whistling through the louvres and nearly taking away the breath, the belfry is reached, and a sudden and loud dong alarms us, but our nerves are reassured as we realise that it is only

> The crazy old church clock
> And the bewildered chimes.

Amidst the heavy timbered framing hang the bells, fine specimens of casting, in good tune, and with pious mottoes beautifully lettered and ornamented. Caution is necessary in examining the bells, especially during ringing time. Impressions of the raised inscriptions and ornaments are obtained by stretching over them strips of thin narrow paper and rubbing with pieces of thin, black boot leather.

The interiors of belfries are often in a dirty condition, owing to birds flying in and out, and jackdaws and owls occasionally taking up their abode there. By a ladder reaching to the trap-door above, the summit of the tower is reached, and a panoramic view of the district obtained. In the centre of the tower is the flag-staff, whilst a corner is occupied by the beacon, restored and re-lighted at Her Majesty's Jubilee. In another corner is the vane, a metal plate turning on a vertical spindle to show the direction of the wind.

Descending the tower, the church is again entered. In front is the alms box, formed from a tree trunk, securely locked, and having clasps of hammered ironwork. The Church-wardens' Pew attracts attention, having at each end of the seat a tall thick wand painted black, with the Royal Arms or CW (churchwarden) in gold on the upper part. These emblems of authority demanded a good deal of respect in days gone by. On the desk-rail are wrought-iron candle-holders. In the spandrels of the nave arches are hatchments, lozenge-shaped black frames containing the coats-of-arms of persons interred in the church. On the floor, fixed to blue stones, are large plates of brass, on which the effigy of the deceased is graven. They are known as "Sepulchral brasses," a form of memorial adopted about the middle of the thirteenth century. Rubbings of these effigies are obtained by placing a piece of thin white paper to cover the brass and then rubbing it over with a piece of black heel-ball, which can be obtained at any shoemaker's. There are also some stone slabs with floriated crosses, an earlier form of memorial. A recess in the wall on the north side was the hermit's cell, formerly tenanted by a recluse.

A small stair leads to the room above the porch, which is termed a parvise ; a small open quatrefoil gives a view into the church, and a fire-place occupies a corner. This room formerly contained a library of chained books, the chain of sufficient length to allow of the book being laid on a desk for perusal. The room was probably occupied by a priest. Descending from the parvise, it is noticed that the walls of the church have been scraped, revealing masons' marks, some faint outlines of " frescoes " and texts on the wall. In this case the interior of the walls being ashlar, the removal of the plaster is justifiable, but the " scraping " process has been carried too far, and plaster removed from rubble walls that were never intended by their designers to be exposed. All the irregularities of these rubble stones have even been accentuated by jointing them in black mortar. Round the walls is a solid mass of masonry, forming a long stone bench or seat, a remnant of the time when there were no other seats in the church.

The wood seats in the nave have beautifully carved ends with poppy heads.

A beautiful oak screen, termed a parclose, separates the nave from the chantry chapel, which contains the tomb of its founder. He erected the chapel, and endowed it with lands, etc., in order that after his death masses should be daily celebrated for his soul. Above are suspended pennon and armour. The chapel contained an altar, and also a "Squint," a splayed opening through the masonry in an oblique direction, which enabled the priest in the chantry chapel to see the elevation of the Host during mass at the high altar. Near the entrance to the chancel is the desk, termed the "Lectern," from which the lessons are read. It is formed of brass, and represents a pelican with wings expanded to hold the Bible. The bird is drawing her blood out of her breast to feed her little ones.

The pulpit of oak has an imposing appearance. It is reached by stairs having twisted balusters, and surmounted by a huge projecting canopy or sounding board, intended to throw the sound of the preacher's voice among the congregation. On the pulpit ledge is a relic of the days of long sermons. It is the wrought-iron frame which con-

tained the sand hour-glass.   Below the pulpit is the
old reading desk, having beneath, the seat formerly
occupied by the parish clerk.   Such a pulpit
is commonly termed a three-decker.   The gallery
at the west end formerly contained the choir of
male and female voices, and the orchestra of flute,
violin, and bassoon.   Now the choir is surpliced,
and consists of male voices only, who are seated
in the chancel, near the organ, which has superseded the instrumental band.

In the vestry are kept the Parish Registers,
Churchwardens' Accounts, etc., which are invalu-
able to the Parish, and in these days of cheap
printing, copies should be made ere the *originals*
perish by neglect or fire.   A framed Terrier suspended on the wall records the possessions of this
church.

The chancel is separated from the nave by a
carved wood screen, with folding doors in the
centre.   The upper part of the screen projects,
and carries a gallery or rood loft, the front of
which has canopied niches that were filled with
figures of saints.   Above the screen is the rood
or Crucifixion, between the figures of St. Mary
and St. John.   The approach to the rood loft is by
a narrow stair in the wall.   Within the chancel are

the stalls, arranged on each side and re-turned at the west end. They are separated from one another by large elbows. The seats are fitted with hinges. Underneath is a bracket, termed a miserere, with a grotesque carving. When turned up it was sufficient, without actually forming a seat, to afford considerable rest to any one leaning upon it, thus being a relief to the infirm ecclesiastics during the long services when it was necessary to stand. At the western end of the south side of the chancel is a low side window, considered to have been the window where lepers assembled outside to hear the service. Three steps lead to the railing across the altar space. The Communion table is placed close to the east wall. At the back is the reredos, enriched with sculpture ; and on either side of the east window are the Commandments and the Belief. South of the table is the piscina, a sculptured recess, containing the sink in which the chalice was rinsed at the time of the celebration of mass ; above was the Credence shelf, on which the bread and wine were placed before consecration. A closet in the wall which contained the sacred vessels was termed a locker. On the south side are the Sedilia, three canopied seats recessed in the wall,

formerly used by the priest, deacon, and sub-
deacon; and on the north side is a sculptured
recess, known as the Easter sepulchre. In it the
crucifix was placed with great solemnity on Good
Friday, and watched continually from that time
till Easter Day, when it was taken out and replaced on the altar with special ceremony. Under
the chancel was the crypt, a chapel with a stone
altar, the top slab being marked with five crosses, in
allusion to the five wounds of Christ, while a recess
in the altar once contained relics, the bones of a
saint. In course of time the crypt, being disused
as a chapel, was utilised as a bone-house; any
bones dug up in the churchyard whilst making
new graves were religiously taken care of and
placed there. In later times it became the vault
of some local family, and is now filled up with
earth. An important element in the decoration
of the edifice is the stained glass. The earliest
was coloured throughout by oxide of metal fused
with it in the furnace, and termed "pot metal."
The first coloured glass windows were formed of
pieces of different colours, arranged in patterns
outlined by lead, similar to mosaic; afterwards the
surface of larger portions of pot metal glass were
adorned with a dark brown fusible colour; then

diapered backgrounds became general, on which were coloured outlined geometrical figures. Afterwards the windows consisted of subject panels alternating with geometrical patterns, termed grisaille work. Then came large single figures under canopies, followed by greater freedom of treatment. Finally, instead of each light being a single subject, the whole window becomes occupied with one general subject.

It is greatly to be regretted that much church furniture of historic and artistic interest, that was considered to adorn the edifice previous to what is termed the restoration of the church, has been sold or lost. They were relics of the various epochs in the history of the church, as well as examples of the progress of art, and were worthy of preservation. All the objects mentioned in this chapter may not be found in every church we may visit, for much destruction has taken place within churches during the centuries they have existed, some suffering more than others, but each edifice has some special feature, and if examined in the manner indicated, the visitor will find the inspection of an old church a source of instruction and delight.

Early Church Dedications.

By J. A. SPARVEL-BAYLY, B.A.

MORE than once during the past ten or twelve years have we heard a puzzled clergyman say, when alluding to his recently restored church, " I do not know when to ask the Bishop to re-open it ; my church, unfortunately, has no dedication that I am aware of." In answer to this, we have, in our turn, put the question, " Is a fair held in your parish ? because, if so, it is most probable that your church is dedicated to the saint whose festival falls upon that fair-day, or the one nearest to it." That there is good warrant for this assertion is proved by a comparison of known dedications with the dates of the fairs held or formerly held, in the respective parishes Knowing that the pagan English had long been accustomed to hold great feasts and drinking festivals in honour of their gods and of dead ancestors, St. Gregory the Great, who was a

shrewd man of the world, directed the day of the
dedication of a church to be kept as a holiday,
that the people might build themselves huts with
branches of trees around the church, and pass the
time in religious feasting. Thus, the parochial
holiday and village fair on the day of the dedication of the church became an institution ; the
sylvan bowers suggested by St. Gregory in his
letter to the Abbot Mellitus being now represented
by the booths and stalls of itinerant mummers and
pedlars.   Still, it would seem that even in the
fifteenth and sixteenth centuries the dedication
names of many of our early churches were equally
unknown.   Can it be possible that some of our
oldest churches had originally no dedication names
at all, but were simply consecrated to the honour
and glory of God ?   It may have been so, but we
can scarcely think it, because in times long since
passed away religious sentiment took the form of
special devotion to this or to that particular saint
—as, for example, that of the Confessor to St.
Peter, "his friend," and to St. John, "his own
dear one." Witness also the reverence of Edward
the Black Prince for the Holy Trinity, as evinced
in his will by the minuteness of the instructions for
his burial in the Trinity Chapel of Canterbury

Cathedral; and it is strange that it was on the Trinity Sunday of 1376 that he, the

> " Sable warrior,
> Mighty victor, mighty Lord,"

entered upon his rest. But perhaps the most striking example is afforded by Henry III., the most alien in heart of all our Angevin Kings, who spent his whole time and energy in vain efforts to recover the Continental dominions lost by his father, John. Henry was, after his fashion, a deeply religious man, and did special honour, by a curious contradiction, to two purely English saints. One of these was Edward the Confessor, whose Abbey Church of Westminster Henry rebuilt in the shape in which we still see it, though it was slightly enlarged by the Renaissance chapel of his Tudor successor, Henry VII. The other was St. Edmund, King of the East Anglians, murdered during the first Danish invasion by the heathen Scandinavians, and duly enshrined as a martyr in the town of Bury St. Edmund's, which takes its title from his relics. After these two English saints Henry named his sons, Edward I. and Edmund, Earl of Lancaster. Therefore, we think it highly improbable that the founders of our ancient churches—" the gates of heaven, the

ladders of prayer "—would omit to associate with
their great and good work the name of that member
of the celestial hierarchy whom they held in the
highest reverence.   To many old churches, other
names than those originally invoked have, without
doubt, been added or substituted ; and especially
so at the time of the Reformation, when, no doubt,
many merely local and historical invocations gave
place to more catholic ascriptions.   Re-dedications,
we know, were also common in honour of the
" saint-name " of some new and popular Bishop of
the diocese.   Mistakes, too, may have arisen
through neglect or ignorance ; and in this arises
one of the greatest difficulties we have to contend
with in forming an estimate of the flow of the tide
of religious fervour in a bygone time, especially as
recent research proves that too much reliance
must not be placed on the " Liber Regis," once
regarded as infallible.   The most valuable and
reliable information on the subject is that obtained
from early wills and similar documents.

It is somewhat strange that during the almost
universal restoration of our churches few, if any,
of the original dedication tablets have been found
or noticed ; but possibly the inscriptions may have
been painted on, instead of incised in the stone.

2

In the north wall of the chancel of Postling Church, Kent, there is a stone containing the following inscription, which we thus interpret :—

xix Kl Septbr	19th Kalendarum Septembris
S. Evsebi cfor	Sancti Eusebii Confessoris,
&c. Hec eccla	etc. Hoc ecclesia
Fuit dedicata	fuit dedicata
In honore sce	In honore sanctæ
Di Matr Mare	Domini Matris Mariæ

We take the word " die " to be understood in the second line, and the " etc." in the third to mean " et Martyris." The sense then is plain and easy. No doubt such inscriptions were as common as the consecration crosses with which we are familiar. Local martyrs and mediæval Churchmen enter, of course, largely into our dedications ; but, as at least eight thousand parish churches were built in England within a century after the Conquest by the Normans, religious houses, chantries, and altars in the already erected churches became the means by which especial honour to the memory of such men as St. Thomas à Becket could be paid, though it is probable that in the case of this most uncompromising champion the Church has ever possessed, the dedications of innumerable parish churches, like that of the

Metropolitan Cathedral itself, became merged in the new title of the Church of St. Thomas à Becket, or St. Thomas of Canterbury, until Henry VIII. so unceremoniously unsainted and unshrined him. Even at Verona, in Italy, we still find a church built in 1316 dedicated to San Tomaso Cantuariense.

It seems worthy of notice that church names in some parts of the country appear to run in groups of almost adjoining parishes, as though some dominant influence had exercised its power upon the early piety of the ancient days in that particular district. And it may perhaps be, in many cases of joint dedication to St. Mary and another, that although St. Mary be placed first, it was often used as a prefixed and expletive term, the last-named saint being the special invocation. In every county of England the dedications were, as a matter of course, most numerous to St. Mary. "To her the eyes of all were raised." Then in most counties came All Saints, so inclusive and so very comprehensive in form, securing, as was believed, the intercession of all, as all were equally appealed to. St. Peter, "the Rock," gives his name both by himself and in conjunction with St. Paul, to many churches ; while St. Paul, unless

united with St. Peter, appears to be rather a rare
dedication, and even when it does appear may
sometimes be a contraction of St. Paulinus, the
Bishop of York, and afterwards of Rochester, who
appears to have been very generally popular.   It
appears somewhat strange that so many of our old
churches should be dedicated to St. Andrew, he
being the special saint of Scotland : but he, himself a fisherman, was also the patron saint of
fishermen.   And it will be remembered that the
monastery, founded by St. Gregory, on the
Cœlian, at Rome, was dedicated to him, and that
from it Gregory sent St. Augustine on his missionary expedition to England.   Can it be that
this association had anything to do with the
veneration in which St. Andrew was evidently
held in olden time?   The dedications to St.
Michael are everywhere numerous, and the
churches dedicated to this saint are generally
situated on the summit of some steep and usually
isolated hill.   This invocation is said to be a survival of Celtic Christianity, and it may well be
that the hill upon which a church dedicated to this
saint now stands may in pagan days have been the
sacred hill or mound on which the Beltaine, or fire
of Bel, was kindled, and sacrifices offered in

honour of the solar deity. When the first Christian missionary planted his preaching cross in our
land, he thought it prudent to acknowledge existing
institutions by carving on the four corners of its
pedestal the dragon's claw. As a matter of fact,
he did a great amount of bowing down in the
House of Rimmon—it was, as St. Gregory
thought, necessary. The serpent bore a very
important part in all representations connected
with the worship of Mithra, whose emblems occur
in many ruined Christian churches, and may still
be seen in the interesting churches at Bradfield
and Norton.

But side by side with the serpent cult, long
before the first missionary had raised the cross,
was the worship of the Sun-god himself, for the
Phœnician trader had come, and with him his
faith. The long sea route from Sidon to England
rendered the establishment of a resident colony
necessary, to be perpetually renewed by fresh
blood as its older members died off, for there was
no " run home " for the worn-out tin-trader, however home-sick he might be. Exile was to him
for life, with hardly any exception. Therefore, on
some high hill, from whose summit he could see
the sun rise in all its glory, he would wait to pros-

trate himself before his deity, as in the old days of infancy among the Syrian hills, and there in time he would place the temple of the Sun-God—the place of the sacred fire, served by a hierophant of priestly caste, descending from father to son, and dwelling close to, if not on, the, to him, holy ground. This hill of the Temple would be distinguished by the Celts around as the Hill of the Light. And when Christianity had become more firmly established in the land, what so natural as that the priests should convert the old Temple on that Hill of Light into a church in honour of him who led the Angelic Host to victory in their conflict with the spirits of evil and darkness. The old carvings to be seen on the gargoyles and fonts of so many of our ancient churches—the fancied visages of demons, genii, giants, and dwarfs are merely traces of a heathenism which lasted on into Christian days—a heathenism which Christianity overlapped and absorbed. It was a great struggle in this, our land, between the old and the new faith; but the time came when the missionary pilgrim needed no longer to inscribe upon the symbol of his faith the totems of a worship he had set himself to subvert.

Dedications to SS. Simon, Jude, and Mark

are conspicuous by their absence from our list of early invocations. This is, of course, accounted for by the comparatively late institution of their festivals, dating only from A.D. 1090. St. James and St. Luke instituted respectively in A.D. 1089 and 1130, are, for the like reason, uncommon, although all five were favourably regarded in later days. Churches bearing the name of St. Nicholas are generally found near the sea-coast, or on banks of rivers. Being regarded as the patron of the sailor, the captive, the poor, and of children, this dedication appears to have been everywhere popular. He was Bishop of Myra, in Asia, and died about A.D. 326. The St. Margaret, whose name so frequently appears in the southern and western parts of England, is most probably the legendary virgin-martyr of Antioch, who died in 306 ; but the saint of this name, commemorated in some parts of Yorkshire, and in the more northern counties, may perhaps be the good and noble-minded Princess Margaret, wife of Malcolm Canmore, King of Scotland, and mother of David I. She was born in 1046, and during her life founded many churches and religious houses, and her memory was much venerated. St. Helen, the Christian Empress, figures somewhat uncertainly in our dedications. In some counties, notably Yorkshire, Kent, and Lincolnshire, her invocation appears to have been at one period very popular ; while in other counties the churches bearing her name seem to have been very few and far between. She founded the church of the Holy Sepulchre at Jerusalem, and the Church of the Nativity at Bethlehem. From the circumstance that her son, Constantine the Great, was in Britain when he assumed the purple, Helen, or Helena, was supposed to have been a British Princess, whereas she was in reality the daughter of an innkeeper in Bithynia ; but the British tradition, revived most probably during the Crusading days, made her name popular in England.

The modern prevalence of St. George in church names is greatly due to loyal feeling during the Georgian era ; but, of course, the dedication commemorates St. George, who was martyred in 285. Being a Christian soldier, he became idealized as a redresser of wrongs—the dragon slayer ; —and in the time of the Crusades as the patron of chivalry, and was adopted by the third Edward as the model of Knighthood for the Order of the Garter. Another century may probably see

English Churches dedicated to St. Victoria, there being a saint of that name who was beheaded in 251. The most authentic life of this saint, and the one accepted by the Roman Church, was written by St. Anthelm, an English monk, son of Kentred, and nephew of Ina, King of Wessex. Why churches dedicated to St. Botolph were placed near the gates of towns we know not. But that they were so is proved by the existence of churches so dedicated near four well-known gates of London ; also at York, Colchester, and many other places in the country. The Holy Cross and the Holy Trinity are both late mediæval ascriptions ; and when we find them appearing in connection with early Norman Churches, we may be sure that they have replaced older invocations. Among the Great Churchmen connected with the history of our land, we find the names of SS. Dunstan, Augustine, Gregory, Paulinus, Clement, Wilfrid, Chad, and many others of less importance.

The Norman Conquest and consequent intercourse with France has caused some of the old churches to be dedicated to St. Giles, the French recluse, who died in or about the year 712, a popularity shared to a great extent by the good Bishop St. Martin, to whom Queen Bertha, wife of Ethel-

bert, very naturally consecrated her first church in
Kent. There are some few dedications to St.
Edmund, especially in the Eastern counties. This
must be the generally revered martyr-King, slain
in 870. This Prince, it will be remembered,
was beaten and shot at with arrows by the Danes.
They proceeded to cut off his head, which, as well
as the decapitated trunk, they threw into the
thickest part of the wood of Eglesdene. The
East Anglians afterwards recovered the body, and
buried it at Hoxne, but could not find the head.
While engaged in the search, some of the men, we
are told, lost their companions, and called,
" Where are you ? " A voice answered, " Here,
here, here ! " On going to the spot the head was
found in a thicket of thorns, guarded by a wolf.
According to Matthew of Westminster, "Cum
caput quæendo inter sylvas socii ad socios
clamantes patrio sermone. Ubi es, ubi es ?
interrogabant. Caput martyria eadem lingua
respondens dixit—Her, her, her." As tales never
lose by their repetition, Lydgate tells us the head
of this English Sebastian—

> Never ceased of al that long day
> So for to crye tyl they kam wher he laye,

and, arriving at the spot whence the sound proceeded, they found a wolf holding the head between his fore feet. The animal politely delivered up his charge, which, the moment it came in contact with the body, returned so exactly to its former position that the junction was not visible, except when closely examined. The wolf remained a harmless spectator of the scene, and after gravely attending the funeral at Hoxne, peacefully trotted off to his native woods. Many legends attach to the spot now called the Golden Bridge, where the unfortunate monarch was captured. One is that a young couple had that day been married and were going home at night. The moon was shining brightly, and made King Edmund's spurs glitter. The Danes were all around looking about for their victim, and to save their own lives the peasants pointed out the place where they had seen the glittering golden spurs. The Danes dragged the King from his hiding-place, and at once commenced the ill-usage which was to terminate so fatally. Then the unhappy Edmund denounced in anticipation all who might thereafter pass that way to be married, and for hundreds of years no newly-married couple would go near the Golden Bridge ; and we believe the spot is still shunned by the engaged ones of the neighbourhood. This dedication may sometimes be confounded with that to St. Edmund the Bishop, who was Archbishop of Canterbury, 1234-45, and after his decease was canonized as St. Edmund of Pontigny, though it is very doubtful whether any of our English churches now commemorate that good man. But be the dedications what they may, our old parish churches will ever prove a source of interest, and command the loving sympathy of all thinking people, for there is something in an ancient village church which has a peculiar charm for the mind—something felt, but not easily described. We take pleasure not only in its stones, but in its very dust. Every such building is a page of our National Church history, reminding us of those early Christian days in this land of ours long before the coming of Augustine and his Italian monks.

The Church Porch.

By William E. A. Axon, f.r.s.l.

CHRISTOPHER HARVEY, after passing through the churchyard, looking at the church stile and the church gate, and surveying the church, comes to the church porch :—

> "Now ere thou passest further, sit thee down
>   In the church porch, and think what thou hast seen ;
>   Let due consideration either crown
>   Or crush thy former purposes : between
> . Rash undertakings and firm resolutions
>   Depends the strength or weakness of conclusions."

And a church porch is not an unfit place in which to think of the past and of the future. Like many other things, it no longer possesses the importance it had in former years. No one is either married or buried in the church porch now, nor is it a place where weighty transactions are generally concluded.

An architect might profitably devote a volume to the church porches of the world. The great cathedrals would hold a foremost place, but in many smaller churches the porches did not lack

beauty. What wealth of care and artistic invention was sometimes lavished upon the structure
we may see by the famous south porch of Adel
Church, with its multifarious carvings of grotesque
symbolism. The apex is a demoniacal head, sup-

A DEL CHURCH PORCH.

posed to represent Satan. Underneath is a cross,
then the lamb with a banner of triumph, and then
the Son of Man seated on His throne. To right
and left are images or symbols of the sun and the
moon, and the four evangelists. On one side two

stems are said to be emblematic of the Law and the Prophets, and terminate in four flowery heads for the Four Gospels ; on the other a single stem symbolic of the Patriarchal System, ending in four branches with serpents' heads, in allusion to the Four Gospels and the Fall of Man. There is much more symbolism connected with Adel in " Archæologia Adelensis," by a late rector, the Rev. H. T. Simpson, M.A. (London, 1879). Mr. Simpson's ingenuity of theorising, however, was not sufficiently restrained to make him a safe guide.

We know from many testimonies that in the earlier ages of Christianity the veneration in which churches were held extended to the whole circuit of the outbuildings, and to the land in which they stood. In the ample porches there were placed relics of the saints. There were rich hangings at the doors of the church. Some of silk made for St. Peter's at Rome by order of Leo III., are mentioned by Anastasius Biblio-thecarius. In the porches and at the entrance to the church itself, the faithful not only prayed, but kissed the pavement.

Here, too, was sometimes the last resting place of great kings and brave warriors, and other worthies. Constantine the Great was buried not in the midst of the Church of the Apostles that he had built at Constantinople, but in its porch. In the Greek Ritual, after the priest has perfumed the church with incense, he performs the same operation for its vestibule, for the sake of the dead who are there, and in honour of the sacred images with which it is adorned.

Images are mentioned in the porches of some of the French churches in the seventeenth century, as also is the custom of chanting litanies there.

St. Chad is said to have been one of the earliest to be buried inside the church. He was first interred near St. Mary's Church, Lichfield, but the body was afterwards transferred to St. Peter's, and placed in a wooden shrine, roofed like a house, and with a hole through which the pilgrims passed their fingers and subtracted a few grains of his dust, which, drunk in water, was supposed to have a powerful remedial effect on various diseases.

The beggars plied their trade in the church porch, and might well hope to reap a rich harvest in an age when the encouragement of mendicity by indiscriminate alms-giving was deemed a virtue

The baptismal fonts were anciently placed in the porch, and there also were wells or basins in which the faithful might wash their hands before entering the church, and thus be reminded of the need both for external and internal purity. Chrysostom says that the poor waiting for alms at the church door are the bowls in which the hands of the soul are to be cleansed by the giving of alms.

The porch was the place in which the penitents had to wait, and in which on Holy Thursday the greater part of the ceremony of reconciliation was performed.

Several councils and synods issued decrees forbidding the trial of pleas in the church or its porches, and the number of the prohibitions is in some measure a proof that such secular uses were not unknown if indeed they were uncommon. Fairs and merchandise from time to time invaded the porches in spite of many protests. The Council of Constantinople, in 692, forbade the sale of food, drink, and ornaments in the circuit of the churches, and in support of the rule, adduced the example of Christ in clearing the Temple of its traffickers. But the church authorities found it a hard task, as a long string of ineffectual

3

ordinances sufficiently shows. Nor were church-men always averse from allowing the sale of certain articles, such as chaplets and medals, girdles of St. Francis of Assisi, scapulars, prayer books, images of the saints, crucifixes, etc., all of which were sold close by the precincts of Notre Dame, and many other churches. It was *apropos* of a controversy on this subject that Jean Baptiste Thiers wrote his " Dissertation sur les Porches des Eglises " (Orleans, 1679), in which there is much curious information. That the separation of the religious from the secular has never been complete, is evidenced by the notices of elections, rates, and other worldly matters, which may still be read on the doors and in the porches of churches. At Mucklestone, near Market Drayton, there hangs in the porch a frame containing engravings after Mr. Hedley Fitton's clever drawings of the district.

The church porch was in former days the place often selected for the payment of dowries, legacies, and other monies. There was a manifest con-venience in such an arrangement, for the names of those present could be added to the record as wit-nesses, and, in case of dispute, their testimony would be important.

When the porch was chambered it furnished a place for the sacristan, or for night watchers, who from it could, by looking into the church, see that it was safe from fire and sacrilege. At Malmesbury Abbey Church it was used as a school-house.

Marriages were celebrated in the porch, and there it was that the Wife of Bath was united to the five husbands whom she survived. The marriage by proxy of Charles I. to Henrietta Maria was celebrated at the door of Nôtre Dame of Paris.

The mystic ceremonies of St. Mark's Eve were celebrated in the church porch. Young men and young women went there between eleven at night and one o'clock on the following morning, and watched for the wraiths of those who were to die within the next twelve months.

Such are some of the bygone associations of the church porch. George Herbert ends his moralising in the church porch thus :—

> " In brief acquit thee, bravely play the man :
>   Look not on pleasures as they come but go ;
>   Deferre nor the least vertue : life's poor span
>   Make not an ell by trifling in thy woe.
>   If thou do ill, the joy fades not the pains ;
>   If well, the pain doth fade, the joy remains.

The Lights of a Mediæval Church.

By the Rev. J. Charles Cox, ll.d., f.s.a.

THE mediæval churches of England were artificially lighted in two ways, namely, by lamps and by candles. The lighting of churches for practical purposes, that is to say, to enable each worshipper, if so minded, to follow the prayers in print, or to join in responses, chants, and hymns not known by heart, was a method of procedure altogether unknown. The ordinary or necessary lights for a church would be few and far between. The usual offices were said by daylight, save at the early winter masses. Gilds were in the habit of attending at the late first evensongs of festivals, but then special provision for lighting was made. In the larger quires, where the night offices were kept, the lamp before the high altar would give at least a dim glimmer, whilst there were usually attached two candle sockets to the great lectern in the centre of the chancel, on which lay large copies of the grayle and antiphonar. Every mass had of course its own light, and the great festivals, especially those of Christmas, Easter, and Candlemas had their special illuminations.

Cressets or mortars, which were cups hollowed in stone and filled with grease or oil with a floating wick, were occasionally placed at doorways and other points of vantage. They were specially used at cloister corners and dormitory staircases in the religious houses. A simple Norman example, formed from a small stone shaft, ten inches high, and four and a half inches in diameter, and hollowed at the top into a shallow cup, was unearthed at the 1894 excavations of the cloister of Watton Priory. In some instances several of these cups are formed in a single large stone. Mr. Micklethwaite instances a stone of this character, with seven cressets, which stands on a base inside the north door of the church of Lewanick, Cornwall. Good folk of those days who attended a service in the dark, or darkling hours, would bring their lanterns, and having brought them would probably keep them lighted when inside the church. In the present century, worshippers at Somersetshire churches on the confines of Exmoor were in the habit, during the darkest of Sunday winter afternoons, of lighting their lanterns for the metrical psalm at the end of the sermon, candles being only provided for the minister and the clerk, and in the singers' loft. An old man told us, in the sixties, how he could remember his father carrying his tinder box to church at Wootton Courtney, and *striking* a light in his seat, from which others were kindled.

With regard to lamps, as distinguished from mere cressets or cups of stone or other material, their chief use in church seems to have been in the chancel. Mackenzie Walcott tells us that "at Lichfield, in 1194; at Salisbury, by Osmund's Custumal; at Hereford, in the time of Edward III., by bequest; and in all wealthy churches, by episcopal injunctions, in the thirteenth century, a perpetual lamp burned day and night before the high-altar."

The continual light of the sanctuary lamp before the high-altar, in honour of the reservation of the Blessed Sacrament, is abundantly referred to in charters, ordinances, inventories, and church accounts from the thirteenth to the sixteenth centuries. The lamp in this instance, to the best of our belief, was never superseded by a candle or torch, the chancels retaining them to the end; but in chapel lights, and lights before images, lamps, in most instances, gave way to candles as time went on, for they were found to give a better and steadier light, and could more easily be kept in order.

In pre-Reformation Churchwarden Accounts, the references to candles are at least twenty times as numerous as those to lamps; nevertheless some interesting allusions to lamps can occasionally be found.   The church of Yatton, Somerset, paid, in 1518, 7d. "for hangyng up yᵉ lampe in yᵉ chanselle," and 2d. "for a lyne to yᵉ lampe." Just twenty years later occurs an entry of 1d. "for makyng clene yᵉ lampe in yᵉ chanselle." Much earlier than this, namely in 1447, the same parish paid 4d. for lamp-wick (*lichline vel filo lichinis*).   The interesting accounts of Yatton show that, from 1445 to 1547, the area of the parish was divided into three districts, for the purpose of making voluntary gatherings, and that those who brought in the gatherings were usually termed "Lightmen," instead of wardens. The name doubtless came from the chief expense having originally been the supporting of lights in the church, and this for festival and exceptional illumination, and not for ordinary utilitarian purposes.

The records of Morebath, Somerset, show that in 1528, "William at Pole vel Potter gave his part of beys (bees), that rested with John Morsse at hys departyn, to the store of Thee to mayntayn a lamppe barnyg afore the figar of Jhu, and afore Sent Sydwyll every principall feste yn the ere, to barne from the furste evensong untyll hygh masse be done the morow, the whyche beys ware yn valure at William at Pole ys departyng ij^s. viij^d."

In 1349, the accounts of St. Michael's, Bath, show a payment of 10d. for oil for the lamp, which would doubtless be the lamp in the chancel before the Blessed Sacrament. The clerk's annual fee for lighting the said lamp was one penny. At first sight this sum, representing a labourer's daily wage, seems altogether inadequate, but the payment was a mere Easter honorarium, as we shall presently see, the perpetual light being only extinguished and rekindled once a year.

There are a variety of charters extant of the thirteenth and fourteenth centuries, by which lands or rent-charges were given to churches, both secular and religious, for the purpose of maintaining lamps for devotional purposes, for instance at Chesterfield, Repton, and Dronfield, Derbyshire; at Alrewas, Wolverhampton, and Lichfield, Staffordshire; as well as at most of our cathedral and big monastic churches. The terms used, such as *lampas*, *lucernà*, and *lichnicus*, clearly mean a lamp, and not candle, torch, or mere cresset. Such charters occasionally only specify the providing of light (*lumen*), and leave it to conjecture as to how the artificial light was to be supplied. On the other hand, candles are sometimes specially named in charter bequests, though usually in those of later date. The earliest of these candle tenures that we have noted are two of the beginning of the thirteenth century, whereby lands were conveyed in Lichfield on yearly payment to the cathedral church of a candle worth 6d. and of a pair of candles to the chapel of the Blessed Virgin in the market-place of the same city.

Hooks in the roofs of churches in front of side altars, notably where there is stone groining, may not infrequently be observed; these have served for the cords or chains of suspended lamps. One of these roof hooks may be noted at the east end of the south quire aisle of the cathedral church of Lichfield.

It will probably be a surprise to some of even our well-read ecclesiologists to learn how large was the number of devotional lights in the majority of our English churches. The most remarkable instance with which we are acquainted is that of the parish church of the small county town of Horncastle, Lincolnshire, where there were twenty-three of such lights.

By will, dated June 9th, 1536, James Barton, of Horncastle, left his body to be buried in the south side of the church of the Blessed Virgin of Horncastle, and made *inter alia* the following bequests :—

Itm to the light in the quiere, viijd.
Itm to Sct George light, viijd.
Itm to the roode light, xijd.
Itm to Sct Michell light, xjd.
Itm to the light of our lady of grace, viijd.
Itm to our lady's light in Sct Nicholes quiere, vjd.
Itm to Sct Helene light, viijd.
Itm to our lady light at the high altares end, viijd.
Itm to our lady light at the font, vjd.
Itm to our lady light of the sowthe side of the churche, vjd.
Itm to our lady light on the northe syde of the churche, vjd.
Itm to our lady light in the churche porche, vjd.
Itm to Jesus light, viijd.
Itm to the yong men's light, vjd.
Itm to Sct Jamys' light, iiijd.
Itm to the trynite light, vjd.

Itm to all hallows light, vjd.

Itm to Sct Tronyans light, viijd.

Itm to Sct Xpofer light, vjd.

Itm to Sct Lawrence light, vjd.

Itm to St Leonarde light, vjd.

Itm to St Savyor light, iiijd.

Itm to St Clement light, iiijd.

The churches of Tideswell, Derbyshire, and All Saints, Derby, had, in the fifteenth century, at least thirteen and fourteen lights respectively. Dulverton, Somersetshire, had twelve lights, Winsford nine, and many of the smallest village churches of that county from three to five. And yet a great mistake would be made if we were led to suppose—as more than one historical novelist has imagined—that a night visit to such churches in pre-Reformation days would have found the gloom to some extent dispelled by the twinkling lights reflected from brightly-coloured figures of the saints. Save at exceptional festivals, no light would have been found burning after nightfall, even in such a church as Horncastle, except "the light in the quere." Reservation was not permitted save at the high altar, and it was only before the Sacrament that the light burned perpetually.

With the exception of this choir light, all the special lights at Horncastle would doubtless be great candles, or torches, as they were more usually called. Serges was another word for these great tapers; it was the term mostly used in the midlands. The churchwardens' accounts of All Saints, Derby, for 1466-7, give detached entries with regard to these great wax lights.

> " Imp'mis Sancte Cat'ne lyght ys upholden by gederyng of the candyllyghter and conteneth xx serges.
>
> Itm Sayncte Nicholas lyght ys upholden by the parishe clerke, by his gederyng of Saint Nicholas nyghte and conteneth xij serges.
>
> Itm whoesoe ever ys scolemaster by gederyng amonge hys scholars upholden before Sancte Nicholas iiij wax serges.
>
> Itm vj wax serges before sancte Loy that be upholden by the farrers.
>
> Itm v serges before Sancte Clemente upholden by the Bakars.
>
> Itm v serges before Oʳ Lady upholden by the Shoemakars.
>
> Itm v serges before the Roode, William Walkar one, John Draper another, Thos. Farynton the thrydde, Thomas Payn the forthe, Thomas Bradshae the fyfte.
>
> Itm v serges before the Mary of pety holden uppe by Rawfe Mayre wyffe.
>
> Itm in or Lady Chappell before oʳ lady ys fonde iij serges, William Walker one, Thomas Knolles another, Richerde Baker ye thrydde.
>
> Itm in the same chapelle by some before sancte John baptiste holden up by William Walker.

Itm v serges before Sancte Cristofer att the fyndyng of
Master Willugby, John Farynton, John Peneston wyffe,
William Bancrofte, and Edmund Busby.

Itm iij serges yt Anc' Geyr fonde one before o' lady,
anoyther before Sancte Cat'ne, the third before the
Trinite alter.

Itm ij serges before Sancte Edmunde holden up by the
gederyng of the clerke of Sante Edmund nyghte and
goyng with Sancte Edmunde within the parishes as ye
doe of Sancte Nicholas nyght."

From this interesting statement, it follows that
there were as many as seventy-eight of these great
wax tapers constantly upheld in the church of All
Saints. The whole would be lighted throughout
the great festivals ; those associated with special
saints from the beginning of the vigil to the end
of the festival. and most of them (if not all) during
the daily morning masses as well as throughout the
daylight, when worshippers were likely to be
present. The custom that now prevails in certain
parts of continental Christendom, as at Poictiers,
of the candle-lighter keeping the great standing
lights before special images and shrines burning
longer on market days, probably held good in the
churches of our English mediæval towns.

The lights at All Saints, Derby, before Saint
Catherine and Saint Nicholas, were evidently
crowns or circlets containing twenty and twelve

tapers respectively. It is interesting to find the gilds of farriers, bakers, and shoemakers, responsible for other groups of tapers, and the school-children did honour to St. Nicholas, the patron saint of boys. The images of St. Nicholas and St. Edmund were taken in procession round the parish on the vigils of their festivals, the clerk collecting from door to door for the support of their special lights during the year.

Thomas Lawrence, the candle-lighter, was an important functionary at All Saints, and was quite distinct from the parish clerk. The candle-lighter of that church was responsible to the wardens, not only for the various serges and their proper kindling, but also kept inventories of the jewels, books, and other ornaments of the church. In 1446, Thomas Lawrence and his son report that they have in their charge sixty serges in wax, more or less. These they would be ready to sell for funeral and other purposes, and the sale would be credited to the church accounts. No doubt there would also be perches or light metal stands in front of the more favourite images, whereon the "perchers" or thin votive tapers, for casual and speedy use, would be placed and lighted, and rapidly burnt away after being offered by grateful

worshippers.   When estimating the glare of light
that would often meet the eye, in the daylight
hours, within our more frequented old English
churches, the frequent gleaming of these smaller
and occasional votive candles must not be over-
looked.

But we are reminded by these Derby accounts
of another source of light in our English mediæval
churches, which is usually only associated in our
minds with the actual period of the funeral ceremony.   We allude to the great wax candles,
torches, or serges, that were used around the
corpse.   They were usually carried in the funeral
procession to the church, and were burnt by
the side of the bodies.   The funeral tapers of the
poorer folk, or of those not associated with special
gilds, seem only to have sufficed for the actua
funeral mass and ceremonials, or thereabouts ; but
with the funerals of the wealthy, or more devout,
it was different.   When all was over, by far the
greater part of these slowly burning thick wax
tapers still remained, and they were removed to
the front of different altars or images, where they
were not infrequently removed by special bequests
or by the piety of sorrowing relatives.   Or, again,
in the case of the more influential, whose hearses

were allowed to remain round their tombs or over
their burial places within the church, the torches
that had burnt there in their fixed places were
renewed from time to time, particularly at the
month's end or trental, and at obits or anniversaries
of death, and when once kindled were usually
allowed to burn themselves out, sometimes occupying in the process several days and nights.   A big
and popular church would seldom then be without
the yellow flare of some of these great funeral
lights.

English churches still retain a few examples of
iron hearses.   At Spratton church, Northamptonshire, the iron rails round a beautiful modelled
knightly effigy of the fourteenth century, are
original.   There are the prickets at the four
corners, on which were placed the great sepulchre
serges.

In 1447, there were twenty-seven of these
"sepulchre serges" in the church of All Saints,
Derby, and the names of those who were responsible for their upholding are all entered.   It would
seem then that these quite permanent serges were
kept burning day by day, but not, we believe,
during the hours of darkness.   Certainly, the office
of candle-lighter in such a church was no *sinecure*.

Three sixteenth century wills of parishioners of All Saints, that we copied at the Lichfield probate office, illustrate this use. William Widdonson, 1515, bequeathes "iiij *li* wax to be brent aboute my body in yᵉ day of my buryall." Richard Robinson, 1518, "wyll have v tapurs of wax in the day of my byryall to bryn aboute my body and likewyse in yᵉ sevent day next ensenyng." John Farjnton, 1526, wills that "my ij torches of yelow wax be bernyed aboute my herse the day of my buryal, And after yᵗ I wyll yt one of them goe to the hye alter in All Halowe Church, and the other to Seynt Kathoryne alter. Also wyll yt my litle link of a torch go to the Trinitie alter."

The true sepulchre serge or torch was not made of pure wax, but a considerable portion of resin was added. The proportion of the latter was sometimes astonishingly large ; thus at Tintinhull, Somerset, in 1440-1, the wardens decided to make four immense wax torches. For this purpose they bought 47 pounds of wax at 29s. 3d., and 43 pounds of resin at 4s., and yarn for the wicks at 15d. William Bowle, who made the torches, was paid 2s. for his three days' work, whilst 20d. was spent in diverse victuals then consumed by

4

William and by the wardens while watching him and 2d. for ointment for his hands.

These parochial torches seem to have been intended for the use of those who could not afford special ones for their departed friends, and were probably provided gratuitously. The Yatton wardens, in 1529, "payd for xxviij pownde wexe, wyche made ye torches and ye tapers wyche shall brene ye corse shall be present xviij^s viij^d" as well as 3s. 6d. for 14 pounds of wick yarn, and 2s. for making the torches. Bequests, by will, in addition to leaving money for various specified lights and the sepulchre light, sometimes leave a sum (as at Pitminster and Trull, Somerset) for "the torches," evidently meaning by this the parochial funeral serges.

Nor are we to imagine that because a particular lamp or big serge was kept definitely burning before a particular image that this excluded more casual gifts of a like kind, and these, too, distinct from the mere hastily consumed thin taper, to which allusion has already been made. In the account given above of lamps, mention was made of a bequest made to keep a lamp burning before Saint Sydwell (Cealwold) at Morebath. In the same year (1528) Joan Hillyer gave "a canstycke of lattyn to stand afore Sent Sydwyle, prisse vjd. Afore the wyche canstycke sche dotte mayntayn a taper before Sent Sydwyll trymmed with flowers to borne there every hye and principal fests, this she doth extende to mayntayne whyll sche lyvyth, gracia divina." To the same church, a few years later, gifts were made of two five-light latten candlesticks to stand before certain images.

The county parishes where there were no craft-gilds, had usually, if well worked, brotherhoods or fraternities, often called stores (*staurum* or *instaurum*), which had gatherings for special devotions, and accepted gifts such as sheep, bees, etc., and offerings for these purposes, apart from the usual churchwarden accounts for general expenses. The young men were often then associated for one purpose, and the maidens for another. The maintaining of lights, latterly almost invariably candles, was one of their chief objects. This subject has been recently ably treated of in connection with Somersetshire, by Bishop Hobhouse, in the 4th vol. of *Somerset Record Series*, and by Rev. F. W. Weaver in *Wells Wills*. The particular light that seems to have been most religiously maintained throughout these west country parishes was the All Souls'

Light, or the Light for the Dead, which was beautifully intended as an ever-present memorial to the worshippers of the immortality of the soul, and of their communion with the faithful departed. The following is a list of the various titles by which this light is mentioned in Somersetshire Wills :—Allsolen Light, Alsolen Store, Lumen Animarum, Almes Light (that is soul-light, *pour les amês*), Lumen Elemosinarum (a confusion with the foregoing), Dead Light, Lumen Mortuum, Lumen Mortuorum, Lumen Defunctorum, and Lumen pro Defunctis.

There were three occasions upon which all mediæval English churches were ablaze with light, Christmas, Candlemas, and Easter.

At the midnight mass on Christmas Eve, or at very early masses on Christmas Day, all parishioners were expected to attend, and English wardens seem usually to have made a special provision of candles ready for a general illumination at that season, as is evidenced by several of the early Somersetshire accounts, such as those of St. Michael's, Bath, and elsewhere, and by the accounts of St. Laurence and St. Mary, Reading, etc. Indeed this custom lingered after the Reformation. The accounts of the church of St. Helen,

Abingdon, state, " 1561, payed for four pounds of candilles upon Christmas in the morning for the masse ; " and again, " 1574, payed for candilles for the church at Christmas." There would be no general candlesticks in the nave and aisles, and doubtless the good folk as they knelt would hold their tapers in their hands, whether provided in the church by the wardens, or carried by them from their own homes.

We cannot refrain from quoting a beautiful passage from a Christmas Sermon for Children, by Rev. S. Baring Gould, from the text " I have ordained a lamp for mine Anointed," as it exactly illustrates old use by modern continental practice:—
" Last winter I was in an old German town. On Christmas Day, in the morning at four o'clock, there was a celebration of the Holy Eucharist in the Cathedral. The building was vast, lofty, and solemn. It was quite dark when I went to it, and the wind was whistling through the carved stone battlements, and the snow was falling out of the starless sky ; only a very feeble glimmer shone through the stained glass of the minster windows into the market-place, where the snow began to whiten the ground, and a shivering sentinel paced up and down before the guard-house. When I

got inside, the church was quite dark, except for the candles on the altar, which were burning, for there was no provision made for lighting it. But by degrees the people came in, and each had brought a little wax taper, a little twisted coil of yellow or white or red wax, and the end was lighted and uncoiled as wanted. Little by little, as the people arrived, the light began to spread throughout the vast building from their tiny sparks of candles ; at last the great Cathedral was full from end to end, and twinkling everywhere, down the nave, behind the pillars, along the aisles, in the transepts, all round the choir, with more than a thousand lights. That great multitude was assembled to meet their Christ, to hail Him born of Mary, laid in a manger ; they had come to pray to their Christ, to sing praises to their Christ, to kneel to, to adore their Christ, and for their Christ they had prepared their feeble lights." In this picture, *mutatis mutandis*, we get a life-like glimpse of our English churches on early Christmas morn in the olden days. One of the good old names for Christmas Day, throughout the Western church, was the Feast of Lights.

The Feast of the Purification of the Blessed Virgin, February 2nd, was the next occasion when

our churches blazed with light, a custom that from
early days gave to the festival the common name
of Candlemas. A proclamation of 30 Henry
VIII., concerning rites and ceremonies of the
church, says :—" On Candelmas Daye it shall be
declared that the bearing of candels is done in the
memorie of Christe, the spirituall lyghte, whom
Simeon dyd prophecye, as it is redde in the
churche that day." Everyone was in the habit
of bringing a candle or taper to church on that
day. They were blessed by the priest and
sprinkled with holy water, and returned lighted to
the people. They were held lighted in the hand
at high mass. After the service they were taken
home and termed holy candles. It was usual to
light them in the house, as a protective during
thunder storms, and also when any lay a-dying.
There is a curious reference to this latter custom
in one of Bishop Latimer's sermons, wherein he
records how, soon after he had taken his Master of
Arts degree, he was called in to a relative who
was very ill, and who died just as he entered the
house. His cousin, who had been in charge of
the sick man, upbraided him much, and told him
she thought his learning worthless, because he did
not know how to bless the corpse with the holy

candle. In addition to the candles borne by the congregation at this feast, special provision for lighting (but in the day time at mass) was made by the wardens. Several of the Somersetshire and other early warden accounts, contain entries relative to two tapers purposely made for Candlemas, but the more usual particular feature, which occurs in most of these parishes year after year, was the making of the trendell, trindell, or trendyll. Originally the trindle (of our word trundle, to roll) seems to have been a roll or coil of thin wax taper, but it afterwards signified a kind of chandelier or series of circular, graduated wheels, attached horizontally to a pole, and often suspended by a cord from the roof; small tapers were fixed to the outer margins of the wheels. There are many entries about it at St. Laurence's, Reading, such as 13s. 4d. for supplying the trendyll with lights, and "payed for the tymber trendle for Candlemas Day iiijd." (1539-40). The Tintinhull wardens had to give, in 1465-6, 6s. 4d. for a new trendell, the old one having caught fire and been burnt. We have not met with any clear evidence about it, but we believe the trendell was usually suspended in the nave in front of the rood, and not in the chancel.

On Maunday Thursday, the Sepulchre, which was sometimes a stone structure, but more usually a movable one of wood, was prepared on the north side of the sanctuary. Late in the evening, or early on Good Friday, the altar was stripped, and the Reserved Sacrament was removed from the tabernacle or pyx, on or over the altar, and placed in the Sepulchre. The perpetual lamp before the Sacrament was taken down and affixed to a stand (often of considerable magnitude and beauty) in front of the Sepulchre. Other lights were frequently kindled at the same place, and the Sepulchre was solemnly watched from the time of its erection until the dawn of Easter, when the Host was replaced upon or over the altar. This watching the Sepulchre was a paid service usually done by two men, probably serving in watches alternately, and entries for their payment occur in almost every known churchwardens' book of pre-Reformation date. This watching had its utilitarian advantage as well as its symbolic signification, for it became customary to offer a great number of tapers to be burnt before the Sepulchre, so that it would be necessary to have someone on the spot night and day, for fear of fire, and to see to the frequent extinguishing or renewal of the smaller lights. One of the most foolish of all the foolish reasons given as an explanation of "low-side windows," is that they were used for watchers of the Sepulchre lights, and hence certain wise-acres at the beginning of the Gothic revival gave to them the ridiculous name of lychnoscopes! As if in our damp English climate the watchers would stop outside in the churchyards to see if the lights were properly burning!

On Easter Eve the perpetual light that had been removed to the front of the Sepulchre, and all other lights there, or that there might per-chance happen to be anywhere else in the church, were solemnly extinguished. The hallowed or holy fire was then kindled in the church porch by means of a crystal or burning glass if the sun was bright, and if not by a new flint and steel. This fire was blessed by the priest, and from it was first kindled the great Paschal Candle, and afterwards the perpetual lamp, and other lamps or candles in the church according as light was required. The devout had let their hearth fires die out at home, and hastened to the church to obtain fresh light from the hallowed fire for their renewal. The immense size of the Paschal Candle has often been explained; in some of our cathedral and abbey churches it was simply colossal, the one for the abbey church of Westminster weighing 300 pounds. Fifteen pounds was a usual weight for one of our smaller English country parish churches. This great taper, which was placed close to the altar, was always burnt in English churches throughout the octave of Easter, at matins, mass, and vespers, and sometimes it appears to have been kept alight continuously, and down to Holy Thursday. At the same time that the Paschal Candle was made, the font taper was usually constructed. It was solemnly conveyed down the church at Easter, and seems to have been placed in a locker by the font, to be ready for ceremonial use at baptisms throughout the year.

Much might be written about altar candles and candlesticks, usually only two in number, but that is a subject that has already been treated of most fully in a variety of ways, and everyone knows that the invariable use for centuries was to have lighted candles at the time of mass. Remarks explanatory of the English use of tenebral candles on their triangular candlesticks (with their mystic gradual extinction), on the processional tapers and their candlesticks, or on the lighted lantern carried before the Reserved Sacrament when the priest visited the sick, might be added. But these details, interesting in themselves, and capable of further original illustration, are somewhat foreign to the purport of this article.

Brief mention must, however, be made of the lights of the rood loft, which were often so numerous as to give to the rood-beam the *alias* of the candle-beam. Entries abound in early accounts proving that on festivals the rood-beam was often a glow of light, being supplied with a continuous line of candle-sockets, and occasionally branched lights. Pages might be filled with extracts as to the methods and manner of lighting the rood loft at different seasons, and at various ceremonials, not a few of which have never appeared in print. A single quotation shall, however, suffice, as the subject has been so often treated of, and it is taken from Mr. Kerry's interesting book on St. Laurence's, Reading :—

"1506, It. payed for sysis (small wax tapers) to the holy (holly) bush at Christmas, ixd.

Paid Macrell for an holy bush before the roode, ijd."

Is not this a forerunner of the Christmas tree ? A holly bush covered with lighted tapers and suspended at Christmastide in front of the rood !

In conclusion, a few words may be given with regard to the changes in lights at the time of the Reformation. The injunctions of Henry VIII., issued in 1538, ordered that "they should suffer from henceforth no candles, tapers, or images of wax to be set before any image or picture, but only the light that commonly goeth across the church by the rood loft, the light before the Sacrament of the altar, and the light about the sepulchre which for the adorning of the church and divine service they shall suffer to remain."

The injunctions of 1547 order the retention of "two lights upon the high altar before the Sacrament," excluding all else. The visitation articles of Archbishop Cranmer of this year inquire "whether they suffer any torches, candles, tapers, or any other lights to be in our churches, but only two lights on the high altar."

Bishop Bale, in *The Image of Both Churches*, inveighs against "The continual light of lamps before the high altar, the burning cressets at triumphs in the night, the torches at burials and solemn processions, tapers at high masses, and the candles at offerings."

Lights seem to be literally a burning question with the reformers. In the zealot Tyndale's *Answer to Sir Thomas More's Dialogue*, occurs the following : " When thou stickest up a candle before the image, thou mightest with as good reason make an hollow belly in the image and pour in meat and drink ; for as the saint neither eateth nor drinketh, so hath he no bodily eyes to delight in the light of a candle."

But in another place the same writer gives a sensible explanation of the origin of this custom, which no one can gainsay :—" Lights were sticked before the memorials of the saints at the beginning, to be a ceremony to put us in remembrance that we so praised the saints, and boasted their livings, that we followed their examples in our deeds, as Christ saith, ' Let your light so shine before men, that they see your good works, and glorify your Father which is in heaven.' "

This is an ecclesiological, and not theological article, and deals rather in the old customs than their modern revival ; but we may be permitted to point out that the beautiful teaching of lights, as appealing to the brightness of Christian hope, has in recent years regained much of its ancient strength in the churches of our land. The great

festivals in many of our most crowded churches,
both in country and in town (and their number
increases year by year), are marked, as of old, by
the gladness and the glow of specially-kindled
lights at the celebration of the Holy Eucharist.

> "The tapers now
> In rosy morning dimly burn!"

the chancel twinkles with the constantly burning
flame of the sanctuary lamp; and the tall sepulchre
serges once more glow beside the bier,
giving gleams to the mourners of resurrection
hopes.   Although there has been no formal
restoration of the beautiful and touching English
custom, once so universal in our churches, of a
light for the faithful departed, we learn, as these
lines are being written, of a fair silver sanctuary
lamp just suspended in the quire of a Staffordshire church, on which are engraved the words :

> "Oh, ye spirits and souls of the righteous, bless ye the Lord ;
> praise Him and magnify Him for ever."

A traveller from the Continent, visiting England
in the fifteenth century, was so struck with the
festival glow of our churches from candles, lamps,
and tapers that he called it the Land of Light.
There can be no doubt that the cult of church
lights was more closely and generally followed in

England than elsewhere throughout Christendom, and this, doubtless, through a desire to correct the natural gloom and comparative dulness of our climate. The recurrence of this sentiment among us may partially arise from a like cause. May England's worshippers, when their eyes are gladdened with kindled lights, ever see in them but symbols of the Light of the World, and thus, and then only, will our native land be able to claim with true justice, the lovely title of the

LAND OF LIGHT !

Concerning Crosses.

By Miss Florence Peacock.

THAT the cross was in some sense a religious symbol amongst the heathen, long before and after the Christian era, there can be but little doubt. It is said that the Spaniards found it an object of veneration when they conquered South America, where it was used as the emblem of the rain god. What connection there was between rain and the cross we do not know ; but it must be remembered that very little of the actual beliefs of those whom Spain subdued, in the new world, has come down to us. One form of the cross is common upon Egyptian monuments, and was used as the sign of immortality. It has been held that the northern nations venerated the cross in pre-Christian times, because in it they beheld the hammer of Thor, the mighty god of war, second only to Odin himself in power and strength. A modern writer expresses this idea in verse :—

5

" You shall mark your food with the hammer of Thor,
   And think you are signing a holy sign ;
   But the high gods shall laugh, for the symbol of war
   You have laid on the bread, and the flesh, and the wine."

It would be impossible in anything like moderate space to give an account of all the forms into which the cross has been fashioned ; in the symbolic language of heraldry alone there are more than a dozen ways in which it is commonly to be seen represented.   Perhaps the most graceful of these are the *Maltese cross* and the *cross patée fitchée*.

In the present paper we have confined ourselves to an endeavour to describe some of the crosses that were erected in England before the Reformation ; the people of the present day do not realise how common crosses were previous to that date.

Almost every parish had its cross, and it was by no means an uncommon thing for the larger parishes and towns to have several.   We know that at Liverpool there was the High Cross, the White Cross, and St. Patrick's Cross.   There was usually the Churchyard Cross ; this was almost invariably placed on the southern side of the church ; in some instances it was a magnificent piece of work, showing the sculptor's art in all its glory, but more often it was comparatively small and plain.

From the time that Britain became Christian until the Reformation, these churchyard crosses continued to be set up ; it has been computed that at least two-thirds of the crosses were then destroyed. Not only those in the churchyards, but Market Crosses, Weeping Crosses, Wayside or Boundary Crosses, were all included amongst those that thus perished.

The Anglo-Saxon crosses usually had the Crucifixion carved on them. It was the custom at that time to erect the churchyard cross either near to the south doorway of the church or by the side of the pathway which led to it, so that the pious might be reminded at all times as they entered or left the building by the sight of Our Saviour upon the Cross, to pray for the souls of those whose bodies were mouldering beneath the grass at their feet.

Occasionally these churchyard crosses were called " Palm Crosses," because on Palm Sunday it formed a station in the Procession of the Blessed Sacrament ; also after the Passion had been recited at Mass on that day, blessed palms were brought out, and the cross was decked with them.

Most likely these palm wreaths remained on the cross until either very late on the following Thursday, or early on Good Friday morning, when no doubt they would be removed. Henry Bunn, in his will, 1501, ordered a cross to be set up in Hardley Churchyard "pro palmis in die ramis palmarum offerendis."*

The ceremonies at the cross on Palm Sunday were common also in France and Germany. It was not only acts of religious ceremonial which took place at the cross ; many civil functions were performed there. Formerly the mayors of Folkestone assembled the electors to meet them at the churchyard cross on the eighth of September, in order to choose the mayor for the following term of office. It must have been an imposing sight ; the sign that the hour had arrived to proceed to the meeting-place was given by the blowing of a horn.† This horn now hangs over the mayor's seat in the Town Hall.

* Bloomfield's "Norfolk," x. 141, edit. 1809.

† At Ripon the badge of the Wakeman (mayor as he has been called since the Municipal Reform Act) is a very old horn, the baldric of which is decorated with little silver ornaments given to it by the various Wakemen ; some of these appear to be very ancient. Another large horn is blown every evening in front of the mayor's house, and at what is known as the Market Cross, an Egyptian-like obelisk which stands in the market-place, and which no doubt occupies the place where the market cross once stood. An engraving of the Wakeman's Horn may be seen in Walbran's "Guide to Ripon."

When all were assembled, the mayor addressed
them and bade them go into the chancel of the
church and there elect the new mayor, which was
then done.   Whether they again returned to the
cross we do not know.   The Manor Court of
Aston Rogers, Shropshire, met at the cross.

The crosses at Sandbach in Cheshire are considered to be older than any in England, but they
do not stand in the churchyard ; they are held by
authorities to date from the eighth century, and
some even consider them not to be later than the
seventh.   They are too well known to need any
description ; there seems to be no reason why
they should not last for the next thousand
years ; the stone of which they are made is the
Lower Silurian formation, and is practically indestructible by weather or time.   It is by no means
an uncommon thing to find the bases of churchyard crosses yet remaining, and at times they are
dug up by the sexton.   Half the stone into which
the base of the cross had been fitted, was dug up
about forty years ago in the churchyard of
Northorpe, Lincolnshire, but it was destroyed at
the time, or very soon afterwards.   At Bottesford,
in the same county, the base of the cross remains
in its original position on the southern side of the

churchyard, about forty or fifty feet from the church. The cross itself is still fixed firmly in its place, but it has evidently been taken up at some time and the column considerably shortened, and then put back again. At the present time it is only about three feet high. The object of thus shortening it seems to have been that a sun-dial might be placed on the top. The head of the cross has been roughly levelled to admit of this being done. The holes in the stone show where it was attached, but the dial itself has long since ceased to mark the drawing nearer of eternity.

The east of England is much poorer in crosses than the west, but Lincolnshire can boast of one which is said to be unique, and is by some people considered to be the most graceful church-yard cross in Britain. It stands in the churchyard of Somersby, near Louth,

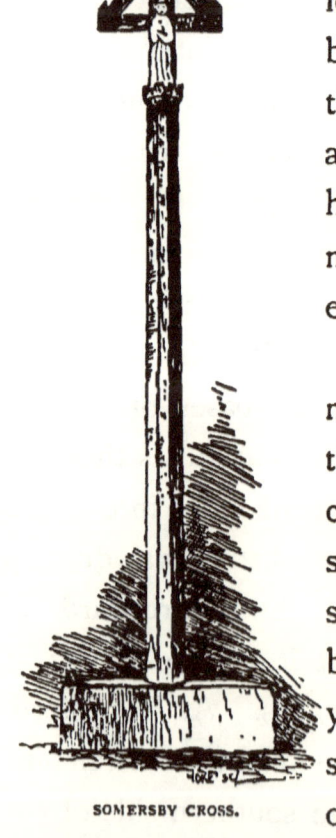

SOMERSBY CROSS.

celebrated as being the birthplace of Tennyson. The beautiful octagonal column springs from broaches which rest upon a square base ; it is fifteen feet high, and is surmounted by an embattled triangle, the top of the shaft having also an embattled head. There is no tradition by whom, or for what purpose, it was erected ; we do not know whether it was meant to keep in the memory of men someone who rests near it, and who has been forgotten these four hundred years, or whether it is a " Weeping Cross," or only the ordinary churchyard cross. There is a good account of it to be found in " Ancient Stone Crosses of England," by Alfred Rimmer. There is a curious custom connected with the churchyard cross at Stringston, in Somersetshire. A writer in the *Ecclesiologist* for 1844 * says, " Until very lately it was the custom of the people of Stringston to do obeisance to the churchyard cross."†

In many parts of England the old feeling of reverence has never died out, but I do not at this moment recollect another instance of the peasantry

---

* iv. 291.

† Sixty years ago, at Kirton-in-Lindsey, Lincolnshire, the old men used to give a pull at their forelocks, towards the altar, on coming into and leaving the church, and the old women curtsied towards it.

paying honour to the cross, so late as the middle of the present century. At Ampthill, in Bedfordshire, there is in the vestry of the church a most interesting fragment of the old cross, which no doubt once stood in the churchyard there. It has on it, on one side, the Crucifixion, which is very general ; on the other, Our Lady, crowned, which is unusual.

Some writers have spoken as though crosses were never erected in churchyards after the Reformation, and no doubt it was rarely done, but we have positive evidence that it was occasionally allowed. The following inscription upon the cross in the churchyard of Fyfield, Berks, is an instance in point :—

This cross was erected
in the yeare 1627
at the expence of
WM. UPTON, esq.*

Wayside crosses are believed not to have been so common in England as they are at the present day in some parts of Spain and Italy, but there were undoubtedly an immense number of them ; there are probably more remaining now in Gloucestershire, Somersetshire, Wiltshire, Devon-

* *Gents. Mag. Lib.*, Topog. i. 156.

shire, and Cornwall than in all the rest of England put together. There were several reasons for the erection of these emblems of Christianity, but no doubt the chief one was that so quaintly expressed in a kind of commentary on the ten commandments, "*Dives et Pauper*," printed by Wynken de Worde, at Westminster, in 1496. The author tells us that "for this reason ben crosses by ye waye, that whan folke passynge see the crosses they sholde thynke on Hym that dyed on the crosse and worshyppe Hym above all thynge."

It was also a practice to set them up on the spot where a murder had taken place, and this is commonly done in Spain even now.

They were often erected in positions suitable for funerals to halt at; the body was placed at the foot of the cross, and the mourners rested and prayed for the soul of the departed. Archbishop Grindell* issued an injunction against resting with corpses at crosses on the way to burial.†

There is a very ancient cross at Lancaster, with the following Runic inscription upon it:

Pray for Cynibald the son of Cuthbert.‡

* Edmund Grindal, Bishop of London; Archbishop of York, 1570; Archbishop of Canterbury, 1575-6.
† Parker Soc. Index, 255.
‡ *Archæological Journal*, iii. 72.

In Ely Cathedral is the base of a cross that was formerly at Heddenham, commemorating the steward of Etheldreda (he seems to have died about 680). The following is the inscription upon it :—

✠ Lucem . Tuam . Ovino .
Da . . Deus . . Et . Requie .
Amen.*

There is the fragment of an ancient cross to be seen close to Doncaster, with an inscription upon it in Norman French :—

✠ ICEST : EST : LA : CRVICE : OTE : D : TILLI :
A : KI : ALME : DEV : EN : FAICE : MERCI :
A . M .

Tradition says that this cross was destroyed by the troops of the Earl of Manchester, either on their way to, or as they came from, the battle of Marston Moor; if there be any truth in the story, it would be most likely to have taken place on the return march southwards. The Parliamentary general was in a great hurry on his way to the north, and however much their zeal against signs and symbols might lead the Puritan soldiers under him to desire to pause and demolish any work of art which lay in their line of march, it

* *Rock*, "The Church of Our Fathers," vol. iii. part i. 18.

is very unlikely that they would have been allowed to waste valuable time by doing so at that juncture.

Near Cambridge once stood a wayside cross, asking the prayers of the passers-by for one Evrard :—

> Quisquis es Eurardi memor esto Bechensis, et ora
> Liber ut ad requiem transeat absque mora.*

Certain crosses seem to have been objects of devotion to various trades or professions. The cross at Kings Weston, Gloucestershire, stood near the Severn, and was an object of great reverence to sailors. After returning from a voyage they visited it, to give thanks for being brought home, and before they again sailed, to pray that they might return in safety.

Wayside crosses, besides being memorials of some person or event, or objects of especial devotion to some class of people, were often used as meeting-places. There is a local tradition which says that the base of a mediæval cross raised on octagonal steps, which yet remains, half-way between York and Fulford, a village about a mile and a-half to the south of that city, was used as a place of meeting between the townsfolk and the

* Leland's " Collectanea," ii. 438.

country people during the Plague in 1665. That it was so used during the cholera in 1833 we know. Those who had market produce of any kind to dispose of, placed their goods on the steps, and when the bargains were concluded, the purchasers in their turn laid the money there, so that none needed to touch each other. There can be but little doubt that the crosses destroyed at the Reformation far exceeded in number those that remained, but the Civil War between Charles I. and his Parliament, attended as it was by an outburst of fanatical zeal, caused many to be demolished which had weathered the greater storm of the preceding century. Many things of interest suffered from the vandalism of the ignorant soldiery, and crosses being considered emblems of Popery, were very hardly dealt with. Over the greater part of England where the tradition exists that any work of art was destroyed from 1642 to 1658, it is stated, and firmly believed to have been caused by, or at least received the sanction of, Cromwell. In some few instances there seems to be evidence that he did allow it, but in most cases he never was near the place either then or at any other time. Unfortunately, the crosses in the west of England have suffered

in more recent days from another cause. It was
by no means an uncommon thing for the farmers
in the eighteenth century, and even till within
living memory, to use them for gate-posts. This
was perhaps done more in Cornwall and Devon
than anywhere else, but the neighbouring counties
can, alas! show specimens of this wanton destruction. The crosses generally to be met with in the
western part of the island are oblong blocks of
granite, generally with a flat circular top, on one
side a Latin cross, on the other usually a rough
sculpture representing the Crucifixion. In some
instances we find the Latin cross replaced by the
Greek one, but this is rarely to be found.
These crosses vary much in size; while some are
nearly eight feet high, others appear only a foot
above the ground. It is believed there is no
Cornish cross with any inscription upon it, save
one, the Market Cross at Penzance. It is said the
following inscription is concealed at the bottom of
the shaft :—

Hic procumbunt corpora plorum.*

The west of England must have been wonderfully rich in crosses; there are five remaining at

* Halliwell, "Rambles in Western Cornwall," p. 29.

the present time in the parish of Lelant, in Cornwall. At St. Erth, in the same county, the cross has a square head, an unusual feature in that part of the country, the heads of the crosses there being nearly all of them circular. Many of these heads have four round holes in them ; when this occurs they are usually named " Four Hole Crosses."

Norfolk possesses several crosses in a fair state of preservation. One of the best amongst them is that in Langley Park. It consists of a single shaft ; the ornamental carvings upon it are very beautiful, and it is in wonderfully good repair. Very early in the present century Sir Thomas Proctor removed it from its original site near the Abbey, and placed it where it now stands, to mark where the parishes of Langley, Chedgrave, and Thurlton meet. In the removal the shaft was unfortunately broken, but it was mended when the cross was once more set up. It is a great pity that it was ever taken from its place, but to put it back might be dangerous, as again the shaft might break. Mr. Samuel Whitbread, the great-grandfather of the late member for Bedford, put up a wayside cross at Cardington in that county, in the centre of the three roads which lead to Bedford, St. Neots, and Cardington. This is a late instance of such a cross being erected before the present revival. Many of the wayside crosses were set up as boundary marks, and they are often alluded to in old chartularies. When by far the greater part of the country was unenclosed, such marks were necessary, and a natural instinct of piety dictated the form.

It would be difficult to say why the east of England suffered more than the southern and more westerly parts of the island by having these memorials destroyed. The city of Lincoln is an example of this. We know Remigius built a cross there, he was succeeded by Hugh de Grenoble, who erected two, if not more, in the city, and from time to time we hear of others. All have perished ; St. Mary's Cross, so-called, being a conduit.

Weeping Crosses were crosses that had either been expressly set up as stations at which to do penance, or those used as such. They must have been very common, for " to return home by weeping cross " became a proverb, and signified that the individual about whom such a remark was made had failed in something in the success of which he was deeply interested, or had in some way or other been very unfortunate.

He that goes out with often losse,
At last comes home by Weeping Cross,*

seems to indicate that the expression was generally
meant to indicate that a person had had a series of
misfortunes in his business or calling in life.

This phrase seems to have lasted as late as
the middle of the eighteenth century.

Ozel,† in his translation of Brantome's " Spanish
Rhodomontades " (2nd edit. 1774, p. 56), says :—
" Making an eruption into Provence, he came
home by weeping cross."

The Weeping Cross at Shrewsbury was one of
the stations on Corpus Christi Day ; the various
guilds and corporations visited it, and there offered
up prayers for a good harvest.   There is a road
outside Salisbury named " King John's Lane,"
leading from Clarendon to Old Sarum.   It is
crossed by another road, and at this point there is
a clump of elm trees.   These trees are known as
" the weeping cross trees."   There can be but
little doubt that on this spot a Weeping Cross
once stood, and the memory of it is handed down

---

* Hazlitt's " Eng. Prov.," p. 3.

† John Ozel.   He was the translator of many French, Italian, and
Spanish Books, amongst the rest, of " Don Quixote," and the works of
Rabelais and Molière.   Pope alluded to him somewhat unfavourably in
" The Dunciad," whereupon he drew a comparison between the poet and
himself, by no means in favour of the former.

to us in this manner, though in all likelihood it perished more than three hundred years ago ; but let a name or a tradition once take firmly hold of the hearts and minds of the people, and it dies hard. As will be seen later on, it seems to have been the custom to plant trees in the place of the cross when it was demolished. I have been informed that on some maps this clump of elms is called " Whipping Cross Tree," which is evidently a corruption. There is, however, a very curious instance of the way in which, what may be termed modern myths, are evolved, to be found in connection with this place. It is stated, and no doubt truly, that the London coach stopped here to pick up passengers, and that their friends usually accompanied them to the starting-point ; and as, in the eighteenth and early part of the nineteenth century, a journey from Salisbury to London was not a thing to be lightly undertaken, the partings that took place here were often of a tearful and melancholy kind, hence the name " Weeping Cross," for they wept where the roads crossed each other. Such is history.

Near Islip Church, Oxfordshire, is to be seen a large elm-tree, its root surrounded by stones. This is known as " The Cross Tree," but whether

6

it was a Weeping Cross, or merely a Wayside Cross, we have no means of knowing.

There is a Weeping Cross near Holywell in Flintshire. The Welsh name for it means the Cross of Mourning.* Weeping Crosses must have been numerous; there is one yet remains near Stafford, and there was one formerly between Banbury and Adderbury.

Preaching Crosses were places where sermons were delivered by the preaching friars and other ecclesiastics. There was, until about twenty years ago, an old sycamore tree in the village street at Messingham, in Lincolnshire. It was named "The Cross Tree," and no doubt occupied the place where the cross once stood. Did John Wesley realise, as standing beneath it he preached to the crowds that flocked to hear him, that, as the shadow of the sycamore fell upon him, so on that very spot had the shadow of the cross fallen, centuries before, upon those who then spoke to the ancestors of the men and women listening to him, of things spiritual and the life eternal to come?

When the old tree died, a young one of the same kind was planted in its place, and is also known

* Rimmer, "Ancient Stone Crosses of England," chap. i. p. 14.

as the "Cross Tree." St. Paul's Cross was one
of the most celebrated of the preaching crosses,
not only of England, but of Europe ; what it may
have been like at first we have no means of knowing, but in later days it was a pulpit of wood,
raised on a flight of stone steps, and covered with
lead. The citizens of London formerly held their
meetings at it, and it is associated with many
historical events, the memories of which yet
remain with us. In the reign of Richard III.,
Jane Shore did penance before it. It was in front
of this cross that Cardinal Wolsey sat in state to
hear fulminations against the doctrines of Luther,
and it was here that, by the orders of Henry VIII.,
sermons were delivered to the wondering crowds
in favour of the Reformation. Hither came Queen
Elizabeth in 1588 to attend a service of solemn
thanksgiving for the defeat of the Spanish Armada.
Sermons continued to be preached here, more or
less irregularly, until 1643, when, by the orders of
Parliament, it was demolished with various objects
of interest. The destruction of crosses, glass, and
the many other monuments of bygone ages,
occasioned much ill-feeling, and there still remains
some of the satires written at the time. The following is a specimen of verse of the better sort

that was written to bring the spoilers of sacred
things into contempt in the eyes of the
people :—

They pluckt communion-tables down, and broke our painted
glasses,
They threw our altars to the ground, and tumbled down the
crosses ;
They set up Cromwell and his heir, the Lord and Lady
Claypole,
Because they hated common-prayer, the organ, and the may-
pole.*

Bishop Percy refers to Whitelock's statement,
under the date May 3, 1643, that Cheapside and
other crosses were ordered to be pulled down by
a vote of Parliament, but this order was not
carried out so far as Charing Cross was concerned
until the summer of 1647.†

In his " Relics " [ii. 331] Bishop Percy prints
an amusing account of the destruction of Charing
Cross.   It commences thus :—

Undone, undone, the lawyers are,
They wander about the towne,
Nor can find the way to Westminster,
Now Charing Cross is downe ;

---

* Thomas Jordan, " A royal Arbor of loyall Poesie," 1663.   Jordan
wrote an immense number of books and pamphlets.   He has been called
"the professed pagent writer and poet-laureat for the city."
† " Relics of Ancient English Poetry," ed. 1794, ii. 333.

> At the end of the Strand, they make a stand,
>   Swearing they are at a loss,
> And chaffing say, that's not the way,
>   They must go by Charing Cross.

There are six verses in the poem, and perhaps the one already quoted and the fifth are the best.

The latter is interesting, as showing that the destruction of crosses was general :—

> The committee said, that verily,
>   To popery it was bent,
> For aught I know, it might be so,
>   For to church it never went.
> What with excise and such device,
>   The kingdom doth begin
> To think you'll leave them ne'er a cross
>   Without doors nor within.

A beautiful specimen of a Preaching Cross at Hereford escaped the fate of so many others, and is still to be seen in the Dominican Priory there. Preaching crosses may yet be found at the Cathedrals of Norwich and Worcester, on the north side. It is said St. Oswald used to preach at the cemetery cross at Worcester, but I do not know the evidence for this belief. There are other specimens of preaching crosses to be seen—we know of the existence of many that have perished —and there must have been numbers of others of which no tradition, either written or unwritten, now remains.

Market crosses were to be found in the Middle Ages in almost all towns ; they were generally placed in the centre of the cross streets, and were no doubt intended as places of shelter for those attending the market. The usual form was a vaulted structure, with opening at the sides and cross on the top ; they varied much in size, shape, and detail. Fine examples yet remain at Chichester, Malmesbury, Elgin, Glastonbury, Shepton Malet in Somersetshire, Salisbury, and other places.

Some people consider the Market Cross at Chichester to be the finest specimen now left in Britain—it is certainly one of the most elaborate. It was built by Edward Storey, who was translated from the see of Carlisle to that of Chichester in 1478. It was restored during the reign of Charles II. by the Duke of Richmond.*

Ipswich could once boast of a very interesting old market cross, but, to the everlasting disgrace of those who authorised such an act of vandalism, it was destroyed early in this century. On the summit was a colossal figure of a woman holding

* Rimmer, "Ancient Stone Crosses of England," 1875, chap. v., p. 62.

a pair of scales ; so far as I am aware, there is but one other instance of this in England, Coventry Cross has the figure of Justice at the top, holding a pair of scales also. There is little doubt that these figures were intended to typify the fact that just dealing ought to reign below. Malmesbury Market Cross is in very good preservation. Leland gives an account of it. Market Crosses served a double purpose : the seller looked upon the cross and swore that what he offered was honestly come by and good, and this supplied the place of a voucher.* The Market Cross at Shepton Mallet, Somersetshire, is one of the best examples that yet remain. It was erected in 1505, by one Walter Buckland, and Agnes, his wife.†

In addition to the Market Cross, each town usually had a High Cross, at whose foot public meetings were held, proclamations made, and much civil business transacted. If there were no High Cross, such things were then, as a rule, done at the Market Cross. Macaulay alludes to this in his account of the Mayor of Plymouth, in " The Armada," raising the standard,

* Southey, " Com. Pl. Bk.," iii. 139.
† Rimmer, " Ancient Stone Crosses of England," 1875, ix. 113.

His yeomen round the market cross make clear an ample
    space,
For there behoves him to set up the standard of Her Grace.

We find that in 1529 the play of "Robert
Cecill" was performed at the High Cross, at
Chester, and that it was newly gilded, most likely
in honour of the event. In 1583, Nicholas Massy,
sheriff, "being a godly zealous man," not long
before his death, pulled down certain Crosses
there by command of the Archbishop's * visitors
—one at the Barrs, one at Northgate, and another
at Spittal Boughton.† There was also a Cross
somewhere near to St. Michael's Church.

There is a meadow on the west side of the city,
called the Roodee. In former days, when the
tide rose it was covered with water, with the
exception of a small island, on which stood a Cross,
or Holy Rood. A writer in the *Gentleman's
Magazine*, in 1807,‡ speaking of Chester, says,
" The only remains of any cross at this time here,
is upon the Roode where races are run." The
High Cross escaped the fate of most of the other
crosses in the city in 1583, but was torn down by
the Puritan soldiers in the following century. In

---

* Edward Sandys, elected Jan. 25, 1577-8, died at Southwell, July 10,
1588.

† *Gents. Mag. Lib.*, Topog. part ii. 117.   ‡ *Ibid.*, 1807, part i. p. 313

1804 the remains were discovered buried in the porch of St. Peter's Church, and were taken to Netterleigh House, and there used to form a kind of ornamental rock work in the gardens. They are now restored to their original position, and Chester High Cross once more looks down on the busy life of the city lying below it.

Melton Mowbray had two crosses; they seem to have been placed at the two principal entrances to the town. The following interesting mention of them occurs in an old minute book belonging to the town :—

1584 Itm. The stock stone at Thorpe Crosse was sold to John Wythers for towe shillings and towe pense, and to plante or sett one Ashe tree, or a thorne, and to renewe the same till yt please god theye grow.

Itm. The stocke stone at Kettelbye Crosse wt one stone standing, is solde to Willm Trigge for fyve shillings and he to sett a Tree and husbond yt till yt growe as abovesaid.

The crosses in Scotland do not seem to have been so elaborate as they were in England ; not infrequently they had the unicorn on the summit. The High Cross of Edinburgh stood in the middle of the High Street. It was removed in 1617, a royal pageant then being organised to welcome home James VI. on his first visit to his northern capital after he had succeeded to the English throne; and it was thought the cross would obstruct the royal procession.

So far as I am aware there has been no list compiled of the crosses that yet remain in Britain. The crosses of some districts have been accurately and fully described ; and scattered about in various periodicals and the transactions of learned societies there is much valuable information to be obtained on the subject, but what is really needed is an exhaustive list of the crosses of Britain, arranged under the counties. A short account of each cross should be given, and especial care ought to be taken to record the existence of the bases or fragments of any kind that are still to be found.

It ought not to be difficult to get some resident in each county to undertake this, the larger counties being sub-divided again, and the result of their investigations forwarded to some zealous antiquary who would undertake to direct the whole proceeding, and edit the book. Surely someone might be found at once capable of, and with leisure enough, to undertake this most needful compilation. The bells of many counties have been fully described and chronicled ; in others the church plate has been made the subject of investigation; the crosses have not been so fortunate, but it is earnestly to be hoped that they may ere long receive the attention they most certainly merit.

Misericordes.

By T. Tindall Wildridge.

ALTHOUGH examples of the graphic art of mediæval times which illustrate life and character with fidelity are abundant, the information conveyed by them is not so vast that the sister art of sculpture cannot be considered as not holding equal place as an exponent of the past. Sculpture had by indirect courses come down from the ancients without material break, and it is fortunate for enquirers into the customs and costumes, habits and habilaments, sports and pastimes, beliefs and disbeliefs of the Middle Ages that the spirit pervading Gothic architecture freely admitted and cherished the representation of common and uncommon things as a part of architectural decoration. Chiefly the churches were the galleries of art in wood and stone, and to these we readily turn for precise information on very many points of mediæval life.

On the one hand we have the stately mail-clad figure, rich with facts scarcely to be met else-

where, on the other the sculptured capital crowded
with some mimic scene; there whole choirs of
life-like musicians; here, below the choir seats, a
series of oaken carvings which are, in this church
or that, mines of antiquarian wealth, giving
countless contemporary facts and countless instances of survivals of thought and design dating
from the birth of the Sphinx. These seat-
carvings are the subject of the present study.

They are found in churches having a connection
with purposes beyond the celebration of ordinary
parochial services, and were an essential adjunct
of collegiate and monastic choirs. Being designs,
by some strange freak of continuous fashion,
more or less independent of the object on which
they are placed, they are less conventional than
other decorations; their retired situation also gave
a free hand, though this was a consideration not
greatly weighing with the artists of old, who were
not usually deterred by motives of prudence or
delicacy.

The seats of the choirs of conventual or
collegiate churches, as well as of the smaller
churches depending on such, are moveable,
turning up on pivot hinges, and on the lower side
is a second seat or shelf. This small second seat

is variously known as the Misericord, Misericordia, Miserere, Patience, Subsellium (Greek, Sumpsellion), Sediculum, or Sellette, and it is this bracket rest which was invariably seized by the mediæval wood carver on which to exercise the most unrestrained freedom of his art. There is a popular error, for which the cathedral cicerone of the old school is responsible, that this is an arrangement to keep awake sleepy ecclesiastics, by compelling them to maintain a watchful regard for their equilibrium, and so avoid an undignified descent into the floor of their stalls. The stability of various examples varies according to the bulk of the projecting block and the angle of fall backward, given either originally or at subsequent replacing of the stalls.

The term "miserere," now in general use, was adopted by Britton in 1817, and by Hart in 1846, but it bears on it the stamp of being an earlier half-jocular term for the misericord. It was anciently customary to stand during religious services, but gradually the practice of sitting during a portion of the time crept in, and was the occasion of severe reprimands by the more severe heads of orders. Eventually the secondary seat seems to have become the compromise by which devotees might rest without entire deviation from the attitude of standing. The twelfth century seems to have been the period when the use of the contrivance came to be fully recognized. The seat proper was only let down at the Epistle, the Gradual at Mass and the Responses at Vespers : but the secondary seat was used at the will or inclination of the canons at any other time. In the early part of the twelfth century, the word

THE SOW AS MUSICIAN *(Beverley).*

misericorde is met at the convent of Hirsaugh, in Germany. Peter of Clugny, in 1121, doubtless alludes, as quoted by Walcott, to the same thing in the expression, " scabella sediliis inhærentia." " Sedes paratae " appears to be the English Mediæval term, though the word misericord was well known. Chaucer says :—

> " The spices of misericorde ben for to lene."

No doubt many a canon prone to comfort would

consider the narrow shelf a penance rather than a mercy, and forgetting how far it was an indulgence, would, as he leaned thereon during the singing of the Penitential Psalm or installion, be applying its opening word to the situation in which he found himself. Hence, doubtless, the misericorde became a miserere.

The earliest examples of misericordes extant in England are those of Exeter, of the thirteenth century, and in them knights in armour are a principal subject; those of Chichester are attributed to the same century. Those of Boston, Cartmell, Ely, Gloucester, Hereford, and Lincoln are among the fourteenth century examples; Carlisle, Chester, Darlington, Norwich, Ripon, and Whalley among the fifteenth century; Beverley, Bristol, and Manchester the sixteenth century; Durham and Wimborne the seventeenth.

Misericordes previously vaunted as being without conventionality of subject, are, in one respect, the most conventional of the ancillary ornaments of churches, for they have almost invariably one curious characteristic: the central design carved on the block, corbel, or bracket of the misericorde, is flanked or supported at the sides by smaller carvings, which, in the majority of cases, have a

distinct connection with the chief subject, and
often are a kind of commentary on it. These
sides are always much smaller than the centre
device, and are connected with it by a band, which
is a continuation of its top moulding and often
encircles the side pendants; they are in semi-
relief (except in a few instances of exquisite
foliage designs), and their object is simply to take
off the blankness of the empty space which would

FOOLS DANCING.(*Beverley*).

otherwise be left. The edge of the misericorde
is generally shaped into six facets, with several
mouldings, very frequently including an inverted
crenellation.

It will be interesting to review a few of the
subjects of misericorde ornamentation.

Scriptural incidents are frequent. At Beverley
Minster are shewn the spies returning from the

7

land of Canaan, bearing between them the grapes of Eschol. At Ripon there is a treatment of the same subject ; here the sides are an excellent representation of a fabulous race of men fully accepted as realities in mediæval times. These are veritable "nobodies," being heads with legs attached to the jaws. One has arms proceeding from his temples. In the *Cosmographiae Universalis* of 1550, there is the following passage : " Sunt qui cervicibus carent, et in humeris habet oculos ; De India ultra Gangem fluvium sita," which, like the report of the spies, was a mere " traveller's tale."

Ripon has three other good biblical subjects. One is Samson bearing away the gates of Gaza. The city affords a good example of the walls of a fortified English town, with a square gate and a round corner tower. Within are indicated the roofs of the houses. The proportions of the whole thing, however, are ludicrous, the gates (two half-doors, iron-bound, with hinges complete) being of a size that a labourer, which the sly and triumphant Elder much resembles, could carry with ease. The other two contain the story of Jonah. First is shewn the prophet being cast overboard by three mariners. The ship is the

usual single-masted, rostrumed mediæval galley.
It is well shewn as though seen from above, the
interior of the crow's nest being seen.   The
" whale," a curious sea-creature, is waiting outside
among the carefully combed waves.   The sequel
carving depicts Jonah being cast out of the jaws
of the much-relieved monster ; he has emerged
half-way, and is in the attitude of prayer.   Behind
is the shore, with a few neat trees.   The trees of

FOOL GRIMACING (*Beverley*).

misericordes are the conventional growths of
carefully-ordered leaves such as from Anglo-
Saxon times had been considered the proper
representation.   Gloucester has the shepherds
(mediævally three) marvelling at the appearance
of the star, their dog sharing in the general
astonishment.   The dresses of these are remark-
ably good, all three wearing hoods, and having

also hats, probably of leather or felt ; one has his hat on his head, the other two bearing them slung behind, as was done with the classic petasus. Two have high many-buttoned boots, and all have at their girdles their knives, other implements, and pouches.

Trades and occupations are illustrated in several examples. In Beverley Minster is a good instance, in which both sides and centre are occupied by the figures of sculptors or carvers, with aprons complete. The best of such, however, is a figure known as the Wellingborough Shoemaker, though it is perhaps to be doubted whether he is not of some other trade, the object on which he is engaged being a tudor rose. He has on his knee-board, however, seven tools, including an awl, a hammer, several chisels, or other cutting instruments. Allied to trades are the carvings dealing with the ever popular subject of ale. At Ludlow an ale-drawer is filling a flagon from a barrel of somewhat the same capacity. At Wellingborough an ale-wife is preparing to pour ale from a jug into a horn cup, but first, apparently, asks a boorish-looking customer for his money. This is evidently not ready, for he scratches his head in perplexity, and both their faces are turned aside

as though for the utterance of *sotto voce* remarks
suited to the occasion. The Ludlow series
also tells the dreadful end of the fraudulent
ale-wife. She is shewn entirely naked, except
for the horned head-dress, and is carried
in an unconventional manner on the back
of a scaly demon. In her hand is her false
measure. Another demon gleefully greets her
with a tune on the bagpipes. At one side a

SHOEMAKER (*Wellingborough*).

third demon is reading from a scroll, which is
presumably either one of her bills, or a list of her
enormities. The common practice of women
keeping ale-houses was productive of much evil,
and they were a constant subject for the satirist
in mediæval times. In the reign of Elizabeth it
became a frequent town's ordinance that ale-
houses be no longer kept by women.

In misereres we find the material form of Hell, so widely believed in during the middle ages, well illustrated. "Hell's Mouth" is shewn, here as elsewhere in church ornament, as the yawning mouth of a dragon, horrid with teeth. There are scenes in many manuscripts very similar to the condemnation of the Ludlow ale-wife, though without the allusions to the trade of the overtaken one; the nearest approach to it in another carving is an elaborate stone sculpture over the south transept doorway of Lincoln Cathedral.

The demons are such as are found in the accepted forms of the greater and the lesser embodiments of pure evil. Lineal descendant of the ancient satyr, the mediæval demon was a man with the legs and feet of a goat, and all the propensities towards mirthful mischief and hilarious abandon characteristic of his classic prototype. The idea of the bad hob-goblin of Saxon-English folk-lore fell in well with the design thus perpetuated by the monks, and the fact that evil is almost invariably represented under ludicrous forms, is probably due to the reflection that good men could afford to laugh; that the demons enjoyed a thousand humorous antics while burning or otherwise tormenting their victims, was of course no consolation to the wicked sufferers. In his transition from classic groves to the haunts of mediæval man, the satyr demon became slightly differentiated in form. His horns in some instances have disappeared, but in most have become those of a bull, and his goatish tail is mostly found to be elongated to that of a bull or lion ; or often has the barbed end incident to the dragon form. From the same source, the dragon being a favourite embodiment of evil, is also derived the demon's bat-like wings. To these physical equipments is frequently added a human face set in the abdomen, as in the famous demon playing Luther's head as bagpipes, or more rarely at the knees. The misericorde carving of the demon rushing upon the miser at his money chest, in Beverley Minster, has these traits, while a figure of a goose-shaped dragon in the same series has the additional human face in the breast. It is not improbable that this was an arrangement brought to mind by the figures used by mummers, who inside light mimic structures representing dragons and other creatures, looked out through a hole cut in the breasts. Perhaps there is no form of mediæval dragon which cannot be found in one or another set of misericordes.

One of the most prevalent subjects was the history of Reynard the Fox. It is to be particularly noticed that the incidents shewn in misericordes by no means closely follow the narrations given in the abundant Reynard literature. The fox preaching to the geese is carved in Boston Church, in Beverley Minster, in the great church of St. Mary in the same town, in Ripon Cathedral, and other places. He is also frequently represented in the seat carvings as having laid violent hands on his flock, as at Nantwich, and many other places. Though, however, the details of the fox's career vary in misericordes from the received story, they closely adopted its main ideas. Thus the ape is shewn as a friend and attendant (in the fable, Reynard claims the monkey family as relatives, and makes them useful to himself). In several carvings the ape participates in Reynard's religious ministrations, and carries some of the poultry. In one he is shewn taking the rope from the fox's neck after the execution of the marauder (shewn fully in another sculpture) by a flock of geese. In another Reynard is laid in a little bed, which has four legs, with a drooping coverlet (rather like the meaner sort of modern German arrangement), while the

ape tends him, perhaps after resuscitation from
his hanging. The hanging by geese is shewn
carved among the misericordes of Sherborne and
Beverley Minsters. In the former the sides are
two monks, who look up from their books to note
the execution. In the latter one of the sides is
the fox prowling near to two sleeping geese.
The gallows is invariably the square mediæval
form. In the pulpit scenes, the fox, in some
representations other than misericordes, is shewn to
be uttering the words of St. Paul to the Philippians,
*Testis est mihi deus quam, cupiam vos omnes
visceribus meis* (God is my witness, how I desire
you all in my bowels). Except when in monkish
garb the fox in misericorde illustration is shewn
simply in his natural appearance, and he is the best
rendered of the numerous animal forms attempted.
There is among the fox carvings some of the
evidence that misericordes were, though not copied
one from another, yet suggested by the same
actual designs. The fox at Ripon is shewn
making off with a goose from among the flock ; a
dog pursues him, and a woman runs out of her
house with her distaff, illustrating the old cry of
" The fox is come into the town, ho ! " The same
thing, exactly tallying in description, is at

Beverley, but very differently rendered. Another in the last-named Minster shews the fox being despatched in a manner which would not have been beloved by Beckford ; an archer shoots him as he lies at the mouth of his earth.

Leaving the fox, another misericorde instancing an old nursery phrase is among the same set ; " The Cat and the Fiddle " is a well-known combination, and there we find her playing to five mice who dance before her. There again the popular fantasy known as " the world turned upside down," has its allusion in the shape of a hare on the back of some unnameable animal, which it is driving.

Minstrelsy of every variety is caricatured in misericordes, the tabor

> " When tightly stretched and struck with hearty blow,
> For half a mile you'll hear it as you go,"

the pipe, the viol, and the harp, most often shewn to be played by the sow (an animal dedicated, by the way, to Apollo), are nearly as common beneath the seats of the choir as on the stone arches above. Both at Ripon and at Beverley are carvings of the sow playing the bagpipes to her dancing family. That of Beverley is the subject of an illustration in this article, and affords also an instance of the harpist sow.

A famous carving is at Beverley in "the shoeing of the Goose," also at Cartmel. A man nails a horse-shoe upon the webbed foot of the bird. This is an allusion to a saying which has left few traces, but which apparently has been formerly of common acceptation, "Whoso melles him, what all men does, let him come here and sho the Goes." *Melles* equals "meddles" and may contain a mediæval pun on hammering. The phrase is equivalent to "*Melez vous de vos affaires*," as supplying an occupation for those who have no business except that of other people.

The Feast of Fools was elaborately celebrated at Beverley, and there is a good carving of three fools engaged in a sort of morris dance, with others at the sides, one supplying the music of pipe and tabor, the other with the time-honoured bladder and staff. It is scarcely necessary to enter here upon an account of the great and popular festival which this in some measure illustrates. The sketches give excellent examples of the fool's costume. Fools' heads with hoods and long stuffed ears are also common, occasionally

grimacing, assisting the distortion of features by
the forcible use of the fingers.   In one instance
the fool's-head has two birds perched upon it.

There is a considerable amount of morality
conveyed by some of these sculptures, some being
very complete sermons.   It is shewn at Beverley
how the Devil is on the watch alike for the
miser who kneels before his treasure chest, and
the prodigal glutton, who, in eating and drinking,
runs to excess in the opposite direction.

The monsters of all times are favourite subjects,
and these are among the best survivals of classic
design.   No doubt the nondescripts plentifully
scattered throughout our churches were believed
in to a considerable extent.   The Greek gryphon
ubiquitous as the mediæval griffin, the dragon
under every conceivable form, the dog-headed
ape, the boar-headed doe with a lion's tail, the
unicorn, the mermaid, and other specimens of
unnatural history, are common.   Ripon has
probably the noblest griffin and the most repulsive
dragon.

At Ripon an old story is well illustrated.   Among
a tangle of oak branches is shewn the wandering
Orson, hairy and muscular, and armed with an
enormous club.   That he may not be mistaken

for an ordinary wild man of the woods, he is
crowned with the knightly chaplet of his forgotten
birth. As well as these direct references there
are many carvings dealing with incidental ordinary
life ; the knight hawking, and the labourers mow-
ing are there. Puns are not unknown, and
heraldry has its part; bear-baiting and boar-
hunting are given in spirited carvings ; while
some of the works are elaborate and careful
compositions of fruit, flowers, or foliage ; and
nearly every symbol of the Church is treated
more or less picturesquely.

Thus the ground covered by the subject of
misericordes is as wide as the whole field of
mediæval art, and almost every phase of thought
has its illustration in these quaint carvings, which,
little regarded in a "minster gloom" more
profound than that which enwraps the rest of the
ecclesiastical ornament, invites in every county
the attention of the curious.

Church Gilds.

By Rev. J. Malet Lambert, M.A., LL.D.,

THE "Guild" is now again a living institution in English Church life. Even in the eclectic circles of Nonconformity here and there we see an institution establishing itself under the name which has become popular with the developments of the Anglican revival. Chiefly as a parochial agency for cherishing a corporate spirit among the youth of the Church, but now and again taking a wider sphere, and under the names of St. Matthew or St. Luke, aiming at a national association of those who feel the urgency of some special aspect of Church work or some theory of social duty, the "Guild" bids fair to settle down as a familiar form of religious and social organism.

Yet it bears upon its face the evidence of its nineteenth century origin. "Guild" is most common as a title of the later trade or mercantile association which played so great a part in the England which followed the Reformation. The original was a "Craft" or a "Gylde" or "Gilde."

The "unnecessary and obtrusive u," as it is severely termed by one of our encyclopædic philologists, is a sign of the relation which the modern association bears to its ancient original, though whether we should be justified in going on to say with the same author, that "Guild" is "an obsolete form of Gild," is a question which we will not attempt to decide.

Freeman, in one of his essays, points out the historical distinction between those names of ancient title or institution which are genuine survivals of bygone ages, and those which are the result of conscious imitation or attempts at revival. The municipal rulers of the city of Alby, at the time of the French Revolution, were called consuls; before many years France itself, under Bonaparte, was governed by a consul. But the consuls of Alby dated from a time when the memory of the consuls of Rome was still a living power in Gaul. The consulship of Bonaparte, like the Capitol of Washington, was a thing of imitation and revival. It is not often that the relics of the past, and the imitation of it, thus touch in the same decade, oftener the gulf between them is wide enough to lend a glamour of mystery and romance to the distance. What we mean, then, is that the ancient gild of which we are about to speak was a different thing from its modern useful, but distinct, congener, dating, it is said, from Manchester in 1851.

What was the ancient church gild? Alas, its very name betrays its ecclesiastical association, as it betokens one source of its enduring popularity and strength. The name is but little removed from the Anglo-Saxon for a collection. The plain-spoken old lady member of Society who briefly described the principles of her Connexion as "a shilling a quarter, a penny a week, and justification by faith," went more to the heart of the enduring principles of association than her hearers conceived. Only there was a directness about the form of the collection in old England which is more in accordance with the bluntness of unsophisticated men than the modern rather clumsy attempts to euphemise over the naked fact. It was *Gildan*, to pay, which gave its name to the gild. The other attempts to account for the origin of the term, such as that which would connect it with Welsh, Briton, or Dutch words, meaning a feast or holiday, may be regarded as mistaken. The ancients were strangers to the modern custom of glossing over the fact of a collection by a pretence of a feast. The transition stage between the two is found in the Elizabethan ordnance which preceded the establishment of the Poor Law, namely, that a (voluntary) collection should be made for the poor, but that those who neglected to subscribe should be visited and given clearly to understand that a continuance of their neglect would result in proceedings before the justices.

Few more interesting subjects for students of the religious and social life of the Middle Ages could be suggested than this. As the mist of oblivion is being lifted from the lower social life of those times, we begin to trace the outlines of the customs and institutions which gave warmth and interest to existence. Life for our forefathers was rigorous enough. Shut in by the walls of their narrow cities, or scattered over the sparsely peopled land, violence may have been common, famine was too often a reality, and pestilence was terrible enough, but when we can get a glimpse of the everyday life of the burgher or villager, we see him to be a man by no means soured or cowed. Civic patriotism was vigorous, trade after its kind struggled against the barriers which restricted it, everywhere the Church reared its massive tower

8

in the centre of the community, and round it
gathered the associations which gave the strongest
bonds of union to the slowly growing elements of
society.

The Church itself, it may be said, is an association, one which claims to satisfy the truest and
widest aspirations of men. What room is there
within her boundaries for these minor associations
which detract from the sense of unity which she
is to cherish in herself? The answer is practical.
At the times when she has been the strongest,
and her influence has been most extensive, there
has always exhibited itself the tendency to
develop subordinate unions within. The extensive character of her domain, the catholicity of
her communion, not only leaves room for, but
invites, the natural cohesion in smaller groups of
those who are attracted by mutual affinity or
united in common aims. Hence the scope for
monastic orders, for gilds and fraternities, in the
Middle Ages, hence, too, the scope for the
multitudinous "Societies" which mark the vigorous Church life of our own day.

The present chapter is concerned especially
with gilds in their connection with the church.
But the very distinction itself is redolent of

modern habits of thought. Nearly all gilds were connected with the church, hardly any gilds were solely and purely a part of church organization. All said prayers, all had their lights, all came solemnly to hear mass and invoke the services of the priest. No gild but rested under the wing of some saint or angel, many under the protection of them all. Though devotees of S. Anthony, the gildsmen founded their ordinances "in the worshep of God of heven, and of his modir Seynt Mari, and alle the holy Company of heven, and souerengly of the noble confessour Seynt Antony, with a grete devocion the fraternite was begonne in the toun of lenne (Lynn)." The anniversary days were Saints Days or were reckoned from them. If this constituted a Church gild our range is wide. But as truly must it be said that of purely ecclesiastical influence, still more of ecclesiastical government or control, there was in the great majority of cases, at any rate till late in the Middle Ages, but little. The priest was possibly the chaplain, in some cases one of the founders, in some was expressly excluded, but the gild was the "fraternite" of the good folk themselves. The line between the gild of a craft and the gild of the patron saint of the craft was one which, if it existed in every case,—and it is doubtful,—we at any rate cannot accurately follow. The craft of the tailors and the gild of "ye holy prophete Seynt Jon baptist" were almost identical. The members of the one were probably members of the other.   We have more than a shrewd suspicion that under this "grete devocion" to some of the "armie of heven" the turbulent journeymen or artisans of more than one craft sought and found some measure of that liberty of association which was denied them in a more open form.   If this be so, it was within the circle of the gild that some of these social forces were nourished, which have claimed so much attention in our own day.

Again, nothing can be more plain than that the religious observances were closely interwoven with observances less distinctly devotional.   We know not quite whether to admire or to smile when we read in the rules of the prayers which were to be said over the great tankards of ale in the gild of Shakespere's town.   Who would pray over them now?   Those were days when the water, if we may judge from the notices in city ordinances, was by no means so wholesome as ale inspected by the mayor, and tried by the ale-conner, and when tea was unknown. The *naivete* of the documents is beyond suspicion. As we study their quaint simplicity, replete with shrewd touches of life, we can imagine no smile passing over the face of the scribe who engrossed them or the brethren who gave them their loyal adhesion. Humour was there, but it was the grave humour of wholehearted men. There was then no such boundary line between the secular and the religious as there is with us. Church and nation, parish and township, were one, different sides of the same life ; prayers and feasting, worship, and work, and merriment, alternated without a thought of incongruity or inconsistency. It is the spirit of that bygone world of thought which was imaged in Dante, and which has now passed away before the haunting self-consciousness of modern civilization.

Let us try to picture to ourselves one of these companies of fourteenth century English men and women. For women were there on terms of independence and respect. They, too, brought their great tankards for the ale ; for the ordinance stated that if any sister did not bring her tankard she should pay a halfpenny. But there is no record, so far as we are aware, of either an alderwoman or other female officer, only, "if any brother or sister is bold enough to take the seat of another," another halfpenny followed.

It is the age of Chaucer, and the goodly fellow-ship of the country town determine to follow the example of their acquaintance and establish a gild. About a score agree to join in the foundation—citizens and their wives, and one or two more on their own account. They meet in the hall, or, as we might say, the Parish room of the place, for as yet they have none of their own, or especially if, as was often the case, the gild was founded on a Sunday, it may be in the nave of the Parish Church. Preliminaries being settled, the ordin-ances were drafted, on lines common to the genus, but having distinctive features of its own, for hardly any two of these old bodies of rules are exactly the same.

Each member promised his payment, perhaps charged his estate with an endowment. In Hull it was two shillings and two-pence for each, or for man and wife; but the form and manner of payments varied much. In Lincoln, in the gild of the Resurrection, it was fourpence to the ale and a penny to the wax on entrance, and thirteen-pence yearly. Officers were appointed—an

alderman, a warden, a rector or a dean, a grace-
man, seneschals, six good men, or twelve, a beadle
or a clerk. Their office was hedged round with
dignity, and privileged by double fines ; sureties
were appointed, and an oaken chest, with its iron
hoops and many locks, was provided for the safe
keeping of parchments and liveries, silver plate,
pewters, money, and old world treasure. The
feast days, the mornspeeches, were decided on,
the fines fixed, the objects of the charity of the
gild determined. Each member affixed his seal.
A new interest was added to life. Each member
belonged henceforth to a new social unity. They
were brethren and sisteren. The monotony of
old custom was broken by the expectation of the
procession and the feast, and the consciousness of
the Church's approval, the special patronage of
the presiding saint, and the remembrance of the
charity to the poor, were sweet to the soul. So
the weeks would pass, and on the Sunday after
the Feast, say, of the Epiphany, a mornspeech
would be held—a general meeting we should say
in these days. If it were held in the proper hall,
the alderman or warden would sit on a raised
chair at the end where the chest of the gild was,
and there, too, were the officers, while the mem-

bers sat on the benches below. Often it would
be held in the nave of the Church. Four times
in the year were these meetings held " to consider
and do whatever the welfare of the gild needs."
Everyone then paid his sixpence, or whatever was
the sum due. If he was in default " he shall pay
a pound of wax." " And the Dean shall pay a
penny for every brother he ought to have warned
and did not." But there is some unruly brother
who is inclined to grumble, or the new-fledged
dignity of the president does not meet with the
respect which is its due. A member is " rebelle
of his tonge ageyn ye Alderman, or ageyn ani of
ye gylde breyeren or sisterere." Such conduct is
foreseen and provided for. The rule is referred
to. "If he grucche (grumble) he shal pay a pounde
of wax, or leve ye fraternite for evere more."
Thus good order is preserved, and the " grete
lyte " is liberally supplied with wax. But the day
of festival is at hand, the order of the procession
is to be arranged, the details of the feast are to be
settled. All is done in good humour, and with
serious attention to business, and the members go
home abundantly satisfied. The great day arrives,
and the brethren and sisters assemble " atte hous
that is assignen for the fraternite, for to gone, two

and two togedre, worshipfully to the chirche, with
the aldirman, for to heren messe and evensonge,
and atte general messe for to offre in worship of
the holy martir, atte messe of Requiem ilke for hem
that ben deed," upon pain of two pounds of wax.
Nor were the prayers ended when the church was
left, for " atte general tyme while the drinkynge
lastes, everyche nygt, afore the feste, the clerk
shal stonden up and done pees ben in the house,
while that he says the bedes for the state of holy
chirche and the state of the londe, with the lygt
brenninge that longes to the compaignye." Hear
the prayer said at Wygnale in Norfolk, " Beseche
we ihesu crist mercy, for the pees and state of
holy chirche, for the pope of Rome an the car-
dinals, for the patriak of Jerusalem, and for the
stat and pees of holy chirche, meinten hem and
susten him ; and for the Archbischope of Canterbury, and the Bischope of Norwyche, and for the
Prioresse of Crabous, and for alle the covent, and
for alle Archbishopes, Bisshopes, Abbotes, Priours
an for alle men and wommen of religioun ; and for
the kynge and the quene and al the comones of
this Roialme." Truly, their sympathies were
wide. Into the details of the feast which followed
our accounts do not enter. Familiar to the

authors of them, they had no thought of the
curiosity of those who should come after, and
should have lost the peculiar secret of their enjoy-
ment. The potentialities of the human system,
as we are often reminded, are wonderful, and that
good digestion waited upon appetite the silence of
the chroniclers would lead us to suppose. Steaks
of roasted porpoise, wonderful pasties, swans, pea-
cocks, and venison—all these and more would be
on the board in some of the greater gilds, nor
would the humbler fare of the lesser ones be less
plentiful or relished the less ; for the great tankards of ale had been first sent to the poor,
and the occasion could be improved, with a good
conscience.

We should, however, do grievous wrong to
these good brethren if we should regard their
fraternities as nothing better than clubs for feasting, praying, and jollity. As we have pictured
the gild so far, it was a social union, with a fixed
payment, with a close connection with the
Church, and with periodical holiday feasts. If
this were all, it would be worthy of passing
interest. But there were two features besides
which gave it a place both of greater practical
usefulness and of higher religious and social

significance. These were its functions of charity to the living, and of its peculiar care for the welfare and memory of the dead. In the more recent popular accounts of the pre-Reformation gilds, there is perhaps too much tendency to dwell exclusively on the former of these aspects. The gilds have been repeatedly described, not without reason, as the Friendly and Provident Associations, the Insurance Societies, the Clubs, and the Trades Unions of the middle ages. But it is difficult to say, and probably no generalisation on the subject could be accurately made, whether to their contemporaries they presented the spectacle of institutions chiefly social, or charitable, or religious. The elements varied in their proportions in different localities and in different gilds of the same town. It is with this word of caution that we proceed to say something of their works of charity. For charity of some kind may be said to have been a universal feature among them, and the kindly feeling it must have cherished in the community where it existed must have been a most wholesome element in contemporary society.

But the first objects were ever, and often exclusively, the members of the gild, "especially to them of the household of faith," as the apostle enjoined of old. Take the memorable gild at Ludlow. "When it happens that any of the bretheren or sisteren of the gild shall have been brought to such want, through theft, fire, ship-wreck, fall of a house, or any other mishap, that they have not enough to live on ; then once, twice, and thrice, but not a fourth time, as much help shall be given to them, out of the goods of the gild, as the rectors and stewards, having regard to the deserts of each, and to the means of the gild, shall order ; so that whoever bears the name of the gild, shall be upraised again, through the ordinances, goods, and help of his brethren." If any brother or sister should be wrongfully cast into prison, the gild would do its utmost to spend money to get him out. "If any of our poorer bretheren or sisteren fall into grievous sickness, they shall be helped, both as to their bodily needs, and other wants, out of the common fund of the gild, until their health is renewed as it was before. But if anyone becomes a leper, or blind, or maimed in limb, or smitten with any other incurable disorder (which God for-bid), we wish that the goods of the gild shall be largely bestowed on him." Again, "If any good girl of the gild, of marriageable age, cannot have the means found by her father, either to go into a religious house or to marry, whichever she wishes to do; friendly and right help shall be given her out of our means and our common chest, towards enabling her to do whichever of the two she wishes." Or at Coventry, "If any brother or sister of the gild become so feeble, through old age or through any worldly mishap, that he has not, and cannot earn, the means of living, he shall have such help, at the cost of the gild, that he shall not need to beg his bread." At Chesterfield also the provision was characteristic, "If any brother is sick and needs help, he shall have a halfpenny daily from the common fund of the gild, until he has got well. If any of them fall into poverty, they shall go, singly, on given days, to the houses of the brethren, where each shall be courteously received, and there shall be given to him, as if he were master of the house, whatever he wants of meat, drink, and clothing, and he shall have a halfpenny like those that are sick ; and then he shall go home in the name of the Lord."

At Hull, in the Corpus Christi Gild, the charity dispensed was strictly practical. "If it befall that any brother or sister become, by mishap, so poor that help is needed, twenty shillings shall be granted to him for one year, to enable him to follow his calling. And if he cannot earn the twenty shillings in that year, he shall keep the money for another year. And if then he cannot earn it, with increase, nor make his living, he shall have it for another year, so that he may make a profit out of it. And if, through no fault of his own, he can get no increase even in the third year, then the money shall be released to him." And in the gild of St. John Baptist, it was further provided that five shillings should be given to each of the afflicted at the feast of St. Martin, in winter, to buy a garment. But the strictly business-like character of this charity is marked by the further provision in these Hull gilds, that in each case, except only in extreme necessity, a deduction was to be made to cover the regular yearly payments due from the members to the gild. Charity, too, in a wider sense was nourished. For, "inasmuch as the gild was founded to cherish kindness and love, the alderman, steward, and two help-men," in case of a quarrel arising between members, "shall deal with the matter, and shall earnestly strive to

make the quarrellers agree together, without any
suit or delay, and so that no damage, either to
body or goods, shall in anywise happen through
the quarrel." And if the officials should neglect
to compose the quarrel, they should pay between
them four pounds of wax, or if the quarrellers
will not listen, "they shall pay four pounds of wax."
And, finally, if the officials cannot agree in a
matter of this sort, "then all and every of the
gild shall be summoned to meet, and the matter
in difference shall be discussed before them, and
be referred to them for settlement." It was, in
fact, a common rule that no brother should go
to law with brother, a rule which not only has
apostolic authority, but even goes back to the
gilds of the heathen, which were contemporary
with and prior to St. Paul.

The extent of the external charity of the gilds
is less easy to determine. It was a common,
and possibly we might even say a universal,
practice among them, that on the occasion of
the annual feast, portions should be given to
the poor. So at Grantham, each married
couple or single man, on the day of the gild
feast, was to feed one poor person. There
were also given to the friars minor of the town

who had gone in procession with them fourteen loaves, eight gallons of ale, and half a kid or sheep. We have already alluded to the tankards of ale at Ludlow, which were given to the poor before the feasting began. But there were other and more far-reaching works of charity done by many gilds. The Report of the Commissioners of Henry VIII. reported of the Gild of the Holy Cross, at Birmingham, "There be dyuers pore people founde, ayded, and suckared, of the seyde Gylde, as in money, Breade, Drynke, Coles." And their successors sent by Edward VI. reported of the same gild, "There be relieved and mainteigned uppon the possessions of the same Guilde, and the good provision of the M^r and bretherne thereof, twelve poore persones, who have their howses Rent free, and alle other kinde of sustenaunce, as welle foode and apparelle as alle other necessaryes." This gild, however, was no ordinary one. Founded by the Bailiffs and Commonalty of the town, its membership and influence must have been very large. It is stated that in the year 37 Henry VIII., there were "in the same towne of Byrmyngham 2000 houseling people. And at Ester tyme, all the prestes of the same Gilde, with dyuers others, be not sufficient to mynyster the sacraments and sacramentalles unto the seyde people." At Coventry also we find that out of the goods and chattels of the gild means of living were found for thirty-one men and women who were unable either to work or to find a living, and this at a charge of thirty-five pounds five shillings a year. "Moreover, one of the houses before named is kept as a lodging-house with thirteen beds, to lodge poor folks coming through the land, on pilgrimage or any other work of charity, in honour of God and of all saints. And there is a Governor of the house, and a woman to wash their feet, and whatever else is needed. The yearly cost hereof is ten pounds."

These, be it remembered were the days of pilgrimage, to Canterbury and farther afield, and the popularity of the custom finds frequent illustration in the ordinances of the 14th century.

In some cases a gild brother going on pilgrimage was excused his payments till his return. It was so at Hull. But at Lincoln, " If any brother or sister wishes to make pilgrimage to Rome, St James of Galacia, or the Holy Land, he shall forewarn the gild ; and all the bretheren and sisteren shall go with him to the city gate, and each shall give him a halfpenny at least."

And at the same city in another gild it was further ordained that they should meet him on his return and go with him to the monastery.

Hitherto we have dealt with the gilds as institutions for the diversion and the profit of the living. We have now to add some illustration of their function in the care for the dead. For the world of the departed loomed larger in the eyes of our forefathers than it does in the nineteenth century. Ghosts were real. At any rate they still lingered round the habitations of the living. At Ludlow, in the gild of the Palmers, "If any man wishes, as is common, to keep night watches with the dead, this will be allowed, on the condition that he does not call up ghosts" (monstra larvarum in ducere).

It is here that we come into contact with what was undoubtedly one of the fundamental and vital principles of ancient gilds—a principle which, indeed, was strong in the middle ages, but which was as potent in far more ancient times, and links on the mediæval gild to the collegium of Rome, and the brotherhoods of both east and west. We will first note the universal practice of our English societies : "All the brethren then in the town (of Lancaster) shall come to placebo and dirige if

summoned by the Belman, or pay twopence";
" all shall go to the mass held for a dead brother
or sister" ; " each brother and sister so dying shall
have at the mass, on the day of burial, six torches
and eighteen wax lights, and at other services two
torches and four wax lights " ; " If any of the gild
dies outside the town of Lancaster, within a space
of twenty miles, twelve brethren shall wend and
seek the body at the cost of the gild, and if the
brother or sister so dying wished to be buried
where he died, the said twelve shall see that he
has fitting burial there, at the cost of the gild."
Or in Lincoln, "When any brother or sister dies
in Lincoln, two torches shall be kept burning about
the body until it has been carried into the Church.
The torches shall then be put out ; afterwards, the
mass being ended, the torches shall be lighted
again, and shall be kept·burning till the body is
buried." Or again, " When any of the bretheren
or sisteren dies, the rest shall give a half-penny
each, to buy bread to be given to the poor, for the
soul's sake of the dead." At Stamford, the ordinance is interesting, "Also it is ordeyned that
when any Broder or Suster of this Gilde is
decessed oute of this worlde, then, withyn the xxx
dayes of that Broder or Suster, in the chirch of

Seynt Poules, ye Steward of this Gilde shall doo Rynge for hym, and do to say a placebo and dirige, w^t a masse on ye morowe of Requiem, as ye commoun use is. Att the which masse, the Alderman of ye gilde, or his depute, shall offer ijd. for the same soule ; and to ye Clerk for Rynging ijd., and to the Belman for goyng aboute ye Town jd. The seid dirige to be holden on ye fryday and it may be, and the masse on the morowe. All this to be doon on ye Coste and charge of the seid gylde." But the pageantry, so dear to the thought of the living and the relatives of the dead, was also provided by the gild. It was a valued privilege to know that the gorgeous pall of the gild would cover the departed, that the "hearse" should be put about it, with thirteen square wax lights burning in four stands, with four angels, and four banners of the Passion with a white border, and scutcheons of the same, powdered with gold. For the hearse was not the hideous monstrosity of to-day. The old iron frame in the church of Tanfield, in Durham, over the Marmion tomb, will serve to illustrate the original of which we have to witness the degenerate descendant. For the poor brother there was no pauper's funeral in store. For him, too, the light would burn, and though his kith and kin were gone, his gild brethren would follow him, two and two, to his last resting-place.

It would carry us beyond our sphere to illustrate the similarity—we might almost say the identity—of these observances in many details with those of the gilds of heathen Rome. The funeral chapel on the Appian way, with its arrangements for memorial feasts and its liveries for the gild brethren, presents an analogy with the mediæval gild too close to be accidental. It is singular how the parallelism at times stands out. Take the following two cases :—

ORDINANCE OF LANCASTER GILD OF HOLY TRINITY AND ST. LEONARD, A.D. 1377.

If any of the gild dies outside the town of Lancaster, within a space of xx miles, xij brethren shall wend and seek the body at the cost of the gild. And if the brother or sister so dying wished to be buried where he died, the said xij shall see that he has fitting burial there at the cost of the gild.

ORDINANCE OF THE GILD OF DIANA AND ANTINOUS AT LANUVIUM, A.D. 133.

If any member die beyond the 20th milestone from the town, and his death be fully reported, three members chosen from our body shall proceed to the place to take charge of his funeral, and shall render a true account, etc. But if the death take place beyond the 20th milestone, then (those undertaking the funeral), shall be re-imbursed.

Change Diana and Antinous into Christian saints, change the objects of worship, increase the charitable ordinances of the gild, and the fundamental social principles of the institution have changed but little in the 1200 years which have elapsed. The payment of the fixed contribution, the endowment, the funeral ceremonies, the help to poorer brethren, the rules for maintaining order, the periodical feasts, the gild hall, the dedication, occur in both Roman and mediæval forms. The persistency of these more homely social institutions throughout long periods of external historic change is one of the most interesting of the facts which meet the student of sociology. Whatever be the explanation of the parallelism we are now noticing, whether it be a case of similar causes producing similar effects, or whether there be in it rather a curious example of more direct historic descent, it is certain that the prevalence of gilds, or at any rate we may say of institutions closely resembling them, is almost co-extensive with the beginning of civilisation both ancient and modern.

Still more strange is the irony of fate. It was this feature in the mediæval English gilds, the one above all others, as we have seen, which

reaches back to an immemorial antiquity, and
seemed in its nature indestructible, which was the
chief cause of their destruction. To estimate the
proportionate strength of state policy, mere greed
for plunder, and religious conviction, in the com-
posite forces which disestablished the chantries,
colleges, and gilds in the reign of Edward VI.,
would be at this date impossible. But it is clear
that although we find instances of a confusion in
the reports of the commissioners between the
chantries and gilds which it is hard to believe was
entirely due to ignorance, nevertheless, in striking
at the gild property the reforming party struck an
effective blow at one of the mainstays of the old
religious system. The pageantry connected with
the masses for the dead, obits, and maintenance of
the chantry priests, was firmly rooted in the old
gilds. Plunder there was, but it was plunder.
which achieved a calculated end.

Still we prefer not to think of them as dead.
The image which we will leave in the minds of
our readers is a brighter sort. In the Minster
town of Beverley was a gild dedicated to St.
Elene, the holy mother of Constantine, who
found the Holyrood. At the year end, the alderman and stewards, and the bretheren and sisteren

of the gild, met together on the feast of St.
Elene; and there a fair youth, the fairest they
could find, was picked out, and clad as a queen,
like to St. Elene.   And an old man went before
the youth, carrying a cross, and another, a
woman, carrying a shovel, in token of the finding
of the Holy Cross.   The sisteren of the gild
followed after, two and two, and then the
bretheren, two and two; and then the two
stewards, and after all followed the alderman.
And so, all fairly clad, they went in procession,
two and two, with much music, to the Church of
the Friars Minors of Beverley; and there, at the
altar of St. Elene, solemn mass was celebrated,
and every one of the gild made an offering of a
penny.   The mass ended, and all prayers said,
they went home; and after dinner, all the gild
met in a room within the hall of the gild; and
there they ate bread and cheese, and drank as
much ale as was good for them.   Afterwards
they chose, by consent of all, out of the best men
of the gild, an alderman and two stewards for the
next year; and to these were handed over all the
goods of the gild.   And the alderman and
stewards were bound to maintain two, or three,
or four, bed-ridden poor folks while they live,

and when these die, they must bury them, and choose others in their place, and in like manner maintain them. Lights were kept burning in honour of St. Elene, and any money in hand at the year's end was spent in repairing the chapel of the gild, and in gifts to the poor. At least, this was the account given of themselves to King Richard by the good folk themselves. Peace be with them.

Pews of the Past.

By J. A. SPARVEL-BAYLY, B.A.

IN every parish of England, from Cumberland to Cornwall, the one most important feature is the venerable building designated the Parish Church. This edifice, with its massive square tower, from which

> " ascends the tapering spire,
> That seems to lift the soul up silently
> To heaven, with all its dreams,"

commands the sympathetic respect of all. Some remember with reverence the scenes which have been enacted within its walls in the days that have gone by, and hope that yet once more it will be the home of the ancient faith. All know that beneath the church's Gothic shade the ashes of their forefathers are laid in peace. A strange feeling of tranquil awe falls upon one on entering so holy and so ancient a building. But, unfortunately, to its habitual frequenters it contains within its walls a fruitful germ of envy, and one calculated to utterly destroy a peaceful and contented state of mind ;

for probably more heart-burnings and petty
jealousies have been caused by the position of
seats or pews within the church than by anything
else connected with the sacred edifice, and it is to
these that we now propose to turn our attention.

Ætheberht had given the little pagan Saxon
temple embosomed in thickets to Augustine and
the monks who came with him. From its ruins,
and on the site of this temple, rose the first
Christian church in Kent, and the homely church
of St. Pancras became the type of future parochial
churches. Simple in form, they possessed no
furniture—the altar, the stone cross, and the
sedilia for the clergy in the chancel, being, in fact,
structural parts of the edifice. The parishioner—
rich or poor, without distinction—who desired to
attend divine service, could, on entering the
church, place himself anywhere in the part
designed for the congregation, none interfering,
and there he was expected to stand or kneel the
whole service through. The inconvenience to the
old, the sick, and infirm, must have been very
great, compelled thus to stand on the damp, cold
floor, whether paved with tiles or stones, or, as
was commonly the case, on the ground itself, the
clay having been simply beaten hard.

A stone bench, in some instances, ran round the north, south, and west walls, to which the weary might retire for a while. In Chaldon Church, Surrey, a long low stone seat ran along the wall of the south aisle, until 1871, when it was " restored " away ; and in Acton Church, near Nantwich, there is still a stone bench along the wall of the south aisle. The porch was always provided with benches, where those coming from a distance might rest themselves before entering the building.

No sitting accommodation for the congregation appears to have been provided before the four-teenth century, though it is probable mats were used to sit and kneel on long before that period. In one parish there is a record of " nats " or mats of plaited straw being charged in the accounts ; and we know that straw and rushes were very gener-ally used for *strewinge* the church, and upon these the people may have sat. But it is somewhat doubtful whether originally this strewing of straw or rushes was not with a view of keeping the church clean, the rushes taking the place of mats. When the roads were bad, and villagers had some distance to walk to church, probably they uninten-tionally brought a good deal of dirt into the building. This supposition arises from certain entries in some old churchwardens' accounts, where particular attention appears to be given to the *new pues*.

In 1493, the churchwardens of St. Mary-at-Hill, in Middlesex, paid 3d. for three burdens of rushes for *ye new pews*, and, in 1504, 2d. for "three berdens of rysshes for the strewing the new pewes."

Within the memory of the present writer, the floors of the churches of Pitsea, Bowers Gifford, Vange, and South Benfleet, in Essex, and that of Swanscombe, in Kent, were regularly covered with straw during the winter months. But it is only fair to say that the same family influence was paramount in the five parishes at that period.

In the inventory of the plate and furniture of Worcester Cathedral there is an entry of "three long carpets to sytt upon at sermons." But these were for the *quyer*. Sermons at this time were not the heavy cumbrous discourses of the religious and political controversalists of the Reformation.

The *Gesta Romanorum* was one of the most applauded compilations of the Middle Ages. Its great popularity encouraged the monks to adopt the method of instructing by fables in their discourses from the moveable pulpits then in use, and

thus endeavour to make an impression on the
minds of their illiterate auditors.   Short and interesting as these moral discourses must have been,
the hearers were often chided for their restless
inattention, probably induced by the standing or
squatting position which, through lack of seats,
they were obliged to adopt.   Thus we find Bishop
Bentham in his visitation articles directing the
people "not to walk up and down in the church,
nor to jangle, babble, nor talk in church time, but
to give diligent attention to the priest."   And long
before, even in the fifteenth century, Myrc had
noticed the very irreverent behaviour of those who
lolled about, lounging against the pillars, as perhaps well they might, if the sermon happened to
be inordinately long.   He says in his *Instructions
for Parish Priests*, that men should put away all
vanity :—

> "Ne non in Chyrche stonde schal,
>   Ny lene to pyler, ne to wal.
>   But fayre on kneus they schall hem sette
>   Knelynge down up on the flette.
>
> .   .   .   .
>
>   And whenne the Gospelle red be schalle
>   Teche hem thenne to stande up alle."

With the increase of domestic comforts, the
necessity for seats became urgent.   The clergy

reluctantly had allowed laymen of opulence to
occupy stalls in the chancel hitherto reserved for
themselves, and it soon became difficult to prevent
other parishioners, differing but in degree, from
enjoying the same privileges in the nave, hence
moveable seats or benches were introduced. The
poorer classes still being without either, the body
of the church remained open ; nor was the space
thus left often unappropriated. In 1326, the tithe-
corn of Fenham, Fenwick, and Beale was collected
in the chapel of Fenham, and about the same
time, when the good monks of Holy Island found
their grange would hold no more, they converted
the chapel attached to their manse into a temporary tithe-barn. A manor-court called Temple
Court was held in the church of SS. Mary and
John the Baptist, Dunwich, annually on the feast
of All Souls. Wool was stored in one of the
churches of Southampton. Parliaments have been
held in the parish church of Northampton, and a
law-suit settled in S. Peter's Church, Bristol. As
an illustration of how old customs survive, we
remember a case in Essex, where the non-resident
incumbent came into the neighbourhood, and expressed a not unreasonable wish to perform service
in the church of his parish (Bowers Gifford). The

principal farmer, an ancestor of the present writer, who was also churchwarden, was consulted ; but a difficulty presented itself. It was harvest time, the weather had been showery and uncertain, and the churchwarden was obliged to reply that they would have had much pleasure in seeing their rector amongst them, but there had been a deficiency in barn accommodation, and the church was then full of his wheat.

That moveable seats were a source of danger to unpopular priests may be gathered from the account of a riot which took place in the church of S. Giles, Edinburgh :—"When the Bishop stepped into the pulpit, hoping to appease them by reminding them of the sanctity of the place, they were the more enraged, throwing at him cudgels, stools, and what was in the way of fury." A woman was at the bottom of this mischief, one Janet Geddes, who, like the wretch that burnt the temple at Ephesus, would never have had her name mentioned but for some villainous exploit of this kind. She struck up the prologue to the subsequent tragedy by heaving her folding stool at the Bishop. There are several stools preserved, which each claim to be Janet Geddes' stool so applied. The derivation of the word

"pew" is about as difficult to determine as the
time in which it came into use. Dr. Johnson
gives the word a Dutch origin, implying "a seat
enclosed in a church." Among other explanations
is that ingeniously suggested by Mr. A. Heales,
F.S.A., in his exhaustive work on *The History
and Law of Church Seats*, that Pewis may be a
corruption of Pervis, the Parvise or Paradise,
used occasionally by our old writers to signify an
enclosure. Nearly all the pre-Reformation church
seats in this country are of the late Perpendicular
era. Pews were, however, in common use, long before that time. In some parts of England, it is now
extremely uncommon to meet with a church still
containing ancient pews, or, more properly
speaking, benches, many of them having fallen
victims, no doubt, to the fashion for family isola-
tion in the sixteenth century ; but in other parts,
old pews still remain, even in this present age of
destructive restoration. Sir Thomas More often
mentions them in his discourses. He tells how
men "fell at varyance for kissing of the pax, or
goyng before in procession, or setting of their
wives' pews in the church ;" while Sir Richard
Baker in his *Chronlcle*, gives a long account of a
disturbance in the church of St. Dunstan, London,

10

between the wives of a nobleman and a knight as to the right of the occupation of a particular pew in that church, resulting in a riot, and death and injury to various persons, partisans of the angry ladies. This event took place early in the fifteenth century. We may, therefore, surmise that pews were sometimes restricted to the use of the fair sex.

Lord Bacon tells us :—" When Sir Thomas More was Lord Chancellor, he did use at mass to sit in the chancel, and his lady in a pew. And whereas upon the holy days during his High Chancellorship, one of his gentlemen, when service at the church was done, ordinarily used to come to my Lady his wife's pew door, and say unto her ' Madam, my Lord is gone ; ' the next holy day after the surrender of his office, and departure of his gentlemen from him, he came unto my Lady his wife's pew himself, and making a low courtesy, said unto her : ' Madam, my Lord is gone.' But she, thinking this at first to be but one of his jests, was little moved till he told her sadly he had given up the Great Seal." At the church of St. Botolph, Aldgate, an entry appears in the year 1553, of money paid to a carpenter for " two new pewes, wherein Dr.

Arthur Darsey and his wife are sett." A pew
each! Addison says :—" If our sex take it into
their heads to wear trunk breeches at church, a
man and his wife would fill a whole pew." But a
man and his wife were not allowed to try the
experiment, for the practice of separating the sexes
seems never to have been abandoned from the
earliest period of Christianity down to the present
time. It is said to have been customary in the
time of St. Mark ; and the author of the Apostolic
Constitution says : " Let the doorkeeper stand at
the gate of the men and the deaconesses at the
gate of the women."

St. Augustine intimates that each sex had its
distinct place ; and St. Ambrose, who was always
getting into scrapes, "was once furiously assaulted
in a church by an Aryan woman, who tried to
hale him by his garments to the women's part
that they might beat him." The great Emperor
Theodosius had to leave his seat in the sanctuary
or chancel, and sit without among the men ; and
the Empress Helena prayed with the women in
their part of the church. Females were forbidden
the privilege of sitting in the chancel in the seventeenth century ; and when the laymen invaded
that sacred portion, the women, ecclesiastically

the most obnoxious, were very pertinacious in
their attempts to do likewise.

> " Lewde men holy church wyl forbede
> To stonde yn the chaunsel whyl men rede,
> Who so ever tharto ys custummer
> Though he be of grete powere.
>
> .   .   .   .
>
> Yet for wommen's sake thys tale ys tolde
> That they oute of the chaunsel holde,"

for it was great folly for women to stand with the
clergy :

> " Other at matyns or at messe,
> But y hyt was yn cas of stresse ;
> For there of may come temptacyun
> And disturbyng of devocyun."

This practice of the laity sitting in the chancel
should have ceased when the nave became
occupied with pews ; but such was not the case.
In an age full of mystical significations, when
every part of the church was symbolized, it
appears nothing strange that the division of the
sexes should still maintain.   That the men should
be placed on the southern—the women on the
northern side, to signify that the saints which be
most advanced in holiness should stand against
the greater temptations of the world.   But
according to others the men are to be in the fore-

part, *i.e.*, eastward, the women behind, because the husband is the head of the wife, and therefore should go before her. The extreme simplicity of this arrangement, makes its symbolical character more impressive.

The seventeenth century came, and with it the time when the pews became both comfortable and magnificent.

The patron of the church had always been well seated, the squire fairly so; but now money and position could acquire by precept, license, or faculty what was needed. Sermons of the highest importance in reference to disputed tenets, and the religious and political controversies of the day were preached in country parishes; and rustic priests, who derived but a scanty subsistence from their tithe-sheaves and tithe-pigs, developed the professional spirit in the highest. In the words of Macaulay : " Living in seclusion, with little opportunity of correcting their opinions, they held and taught the doctrines of hereditary right, of passive obedience, and of non-resistance, in all their crude absurdity." The high pew became a refuge for the parishioners to sit or sleep in, where the Puritan could listen to a teaching not sufficiently reformed, and the loyal

Catholic could cross himself in safety, and mutter his aves unnoticed.

The luxury of some pews of this period may be inferred from their having glass windows. At Merstham, in Surrey, until comparatively recently there were pews raised some feet above the cold damp floor, comfortably fitted, and possessing a fire-place and table—by no means an uncommon example. Such pride of place must have been peculiarly offensive even in private chapels. That such seats were well considered and tended, we may readily believe. In the *Booke of Nurture*, by John Russell, A.D. 1420, the following advice is given concerning "the office of a chamberlain, to prepare for his master attending church "—

> " Prynce or prelate if hit be, or any other potestate,
> Or he enter in to the churche, be it erly or late,
> Perceive all thynges for his pewe that yt be made
>   preparate.
> Bothe cosshyn, carpet, and curteyn, bedes and boke,
>   forget not that,
> Then to your Sovereyne's chamber walk ye in haste."

It was this fashion of having "seates or pewes made high and easie for the parishioners to sit or sleepe in, a fashion of no long continuance and worthy of reformation," which called forth the indignant reproof from Bishop Corbet :—"I am verily persuaded," he says, "were it not for the pulpit and the pews (I do not now mean the Altar and the Font for the two Sacraments, but for the pulpit and stools as you call them) many churches had been down that stand. Stately

CANOPIED PEW, BREEDON-ON-THE-HILL.

pews are now become tabernacles with rings and curtains to them. There wants nothing but beds to hear the Word of God on ; we have casements, locks and keys, and cushions—I had almost said bolster and pillows ; and for those we love the

Church." Strong words, but undoubtedly in their time very true.

A good example of a canopied pew is in the church of Breedon-on-the-Hill, Leicestershire. It bears the date of 1627. This pew is in the Ferrers or north aisle of the church, which is railed off from the rest of the building. The Earl of Ferrers is the owner of the pew, but it is never used. It is beautifully carved, and on the whole, is in a good state of preservation.

A pew seems, from the following story, to have sometimes been the eminence upon which offenders did public penance : " These witness in dede will not lye," as the pore man sayd by the priest, " if I may be homely to tell you a mery tale by the way." " A mery tale," quod I, "commith never amyse to me." "The pore man," quod he, "had founde ye priest over famyliar with hys wyfe, and because he spake of yt abrode and could not prove yt, the priest sued him before ye byshoppes offyciale for dyffamatyon, where the pore man upon pain of cursynge (*i.e.*, excommunication), was commanded that in hys paryshe chyrche, he should upon ye Sundaye at high masse time, stand up and sai, ' Mouth, thou lyest !' Whereupon, for fulfilling of hys penance

up was the pore soul set in a pew that the
people might wonder on hym and hear what he
sayd.   And there all a loud (when he had

PEW, WENSLEY CHURCH.

rehersyed what he had reported by the priest),
then he sett hys handys on hys mouthe and saide,
'Mouth! mouth, thou lyest ;' and by and by
thereupon he set hys hand upon his eyen and

saide, 'but eyen, eyen,' quod he, 'by ye mass ye lie not a whitte.'"

We give an illustration of a historically interesting pew in Wensley Church, Yorkshire. The chief part of it consists of portions of a richly-carved parclose, believed to have been brought from the Scrope Chantry, Easby Abbey, near Richmond, in the county of York, the ancient burying-place of the Scropes. On the top of the screen are inscriptions, and "a sort of Scrope pedigree in woodwork." The carving is well executed, the pew was richly gilt and blazoned. It belongs to the Lords of Bolton, and in the tomb under it rest the remains of members of that noble family. The flag suspended above the pew is that of Loyal Dales' Volunteers.

Before the well-cushioned family pew could be reached, a journey in many cases had to be undertaken, sometimes attended with no few difficulties. All the establishment was beaten up, and the lord of the manor marched at the head of no mean procession, carrying his favourite hawk on his wrist, and closely followed by his hounds. The latter, when arrived at the church, were placed in the "hall dog pew" during divine service. One of these pews was in existence, and used for this purpose, at Aveley, in Essex, at the close of the last century.

That the clergy possessed no power to check the freaks of the squirearchy, and if they had would not have used it to the hurt or hindrance of those animals which ministered to their pleasures, is most abundantly proved. It was always difficult to restrain the clergy from the pursuit of field sports from the time of King Edgar to that of Rowland Hill. One of the ecclesiastical canons, passed in the reign of the former, enjoins : " That no priest be a hunter, or fowler, or player at tables, but let him play on his books as becometh his calling." Lord Hermand, the Scotch judge, had a large Newfoundland dog called Dolphin, which used to go everywhere with him, and even to church on Sundays. His master taught him to place his huge paws on the book-board of the pew, and rest his head gravely thereon, like a country farmer. The dog seemed to relish this part of his duty, and when the judge could not attend, went itself to church and devoutly listened. And when there was no service in the parish church, the dog was even liberal enough to attend the dissenters' meeting house with apparently equal relish and

spiritual refreshment.   A Scottish laird, en-
sconced in the family pew, thought nothing of
there smoking his accustomed pipe, and the yelp-
ing cur at his feet would often disturb the parson
in the midst of his most polished eloquence.   But
the social barometer had not then risen ; the
parsons were not as yet the men they were in the
time of Cowper :—

> "The things that mount the rostrum with a skip,
> And then skip down again ; pronounce a text,
> Cry 'hem ;' and read what they never wrote,
> Just fifteen minutes, huddle up their work,
> And with a well-bred whisper close the scene."

As an example of the way licenses for pews
were asked for and obtained, we may mention the
instance of a clergyman and his wife who alleged
that they had lately purchased an ancient house
in the parish, " where, by reason of the situation
and air, she, for her health's sake, for five months
past, and he also do sometimes dwell," and not
having a convenient seat, and there "also wanting a seat for women who came after childbirth to
give God thanks," they offered to build, in a void
place, a seat for themselves and one for such
women.   So a faculty was at once granted to
them for leave to build two pews.   Thus, with a

show of providing occasional additional accommodation to a part of the parishioners, they acquired two new pews for themselves and servants.

The absence of any system in making these early grants will be seen in another case. The applicant, a widow, was decreed to be restored to the "uppermost room in the pew, as before, and her husband's place also to be restored if she should again marry." In another, the court directed the churchwardens to "place Mr. Church, his daughters, when God should send them him, in the said third seat."

The attempt to seat parishioners according to their degree three centuries ago involved very great litigation, and we are sorry to think that ever since pews have been fought for more for the pride of place than as places for prayer.

Man is a creature of habit. It is likely that while many persons would consciously or unconsciously each acquire the habit of occupying a particular place, their neighbours would, from friendly feelings or peaceable motives, be disinclined to interfere, a right by courtesy would be acquired, and this right be allowed on no other grounds by the Ecclesiastical Courts. We take for granted the undisputed right of the patron and the lord of the manor, or his representative, to share with the rector those parts of the chancel which have, by common consent, appertained respectively thereto. Until the restoration of Swanscombe Church, Kent, in the year 1873, the whole of the south side of the long chancel of that ancient edifice was occupied by a magnificently upholstered pew, with table, etc., in which sat, in solitary state, a dignified tenant farmer, as representative of the lord of the important Manor of Swanscombe. The north side of the chancel being equally divided between the rector and the lord of the tributary Manor of Alkerden in the same parish.

While on the Continent the parson is chargeable for the repairs of the whole church, in England he is responsible for the state of the chancel alone, and in some instances not for that. In London, from long usage, the inhabitants claim the right of appointing both churchwardens, and they have the privilege and duty of repairing the chancel as well as the nave, and apportioning the seats in both, but as a rule their authority is limited to the nave.

The claim of churchwardens to appoint to

everyone where he must sit in the church, appears to have been enforced in 1605 against one Lancelot Ridley, who was presented "for that he will not be ordered for his seat in church, being appointed by the churchwardens," and being interrogated on the next court day whether he had done so, "Dixit that he hath not, nor doth sit in it," wherefore he was pronounced in contempt, and suspended "*Ab ingressu ecclesiæ*." Rather a singular punishment, but no doubt a very effectual means of preventing a repetition of the offence.

There might be reasons we know not of why Lancelot would not sit where he was ordered. We have heard of church rats and mice, but a "hungry—." Well, we will give an extract from the churchwardens' account-book of St. Margaret's, Westminster :—

> "1610. Item. Paid to Goodwyfe Wells for salt to destroy the fleas in the Churchwardens' seat, 6d."

Perhaps such presence may have been accepted as a reasonable excuse which, under an Act of Elizabeth, every inhabitant had to make for not being present at the solemn services of the Church. But if some sittings were uncomfortable, we may imagine those provided by the

generosity of benefactors were not so.   Amongst
these we should class the pew erected in the nave
of Little Bemington Church by a shepherd
crossed in love, who, lacking a *memento mori*
inscription, has spoiled the effect of his very
commodious pew by placing a skeleton carved in
wood in the south-west angle, with the inscription :—

> " For couples joined in wedlock ; and my Friende
>   That stranger is ; this seate I did intende
>   Built at the cost and charge of
> >   Stephen Crossbe,
> >   1640."

About this time (1640), the pews were so
arranged in many churches that they could easily
be taken up, and the ground used for interments.

Among the numerous pews of the past bearing
inscriptions, we may mention one at Whalley, to
this effect :—

> "Factum est per Rogerum Nowell, Ann. MCCCCCXXXIIIJ."

The history of it is this, as appears from the
deposition of an old parish clerk given in a suit
in 1605.   A pew belonging to the Townley
family in right of their Manor of Hapton, was
anciently called St. Anton's Cage ; and a dispute
having arisen in respect to places in the church,

Sir Joseph Townley, as the principal man in the parish, was called upon to decide it; and afterwards it was remembered that he had made use of the following remarkable words :—" My man Shuttleworth, of Hacking, made this form, and here will I sit when I come ; and my cousin Nowell may make one behind me if he please ; and my son Sherbourne shall make one on the other side, and Mr. Catterale another behind him, and for the residue the use shall be, ' First come, first speed,' and that will make the proud wives of Whalley rise betimes to come to church." This is simply the sovereign order of the local autocrat, for which no authority but his *ipse dixit* is pretended.

In contrasting the pewed churches of the seventeenth century with the bare and comparatively unfurnished naves of earlier times, we should remember that though the pre-Reformation congregations were for the most part unseated, they usually stood or knelt within reach of benches, to which they could retire in case of illness or extreme fatigue.

So long as the people's quarter preserved its old social usages, and was by turns a court-house, a market-hall, a granary, and a place for such

11

neighbourly entertainments as church ales and
bid ales, it usually contained stacked away in
corners, a stock of boards, stools, and tables.   It
seems to us strange that the sacred buildings
should have been used for any secular purposes,
yet such was the case ; and we are compelled to
confess that the advice given by Seager, in his
Schoole of Virtue, printed in 1557, is still often
disregarded :—

> " When to the churche thou shalt repayer,
> Knelynge or standynge, to God make thy prayer ;
> All worldly matters from thy minde set apart,
> Earnestly prayinge, to God lyfte up thy heart."

The Bishop's Throne.

BY THE REV. GEO. S. TYACK, B.A.

FROM very early, if not even from the earliest, times it has been customary for a special seat to be reserved for the Bishop in the chief church of his diocese. This, as is well-known, has given its name to the cathedral, from the Greek *cathedra*, and even to the See itself, from the Latin *sedes*, both being, in a narrower or a wider sense, seats of the Bishop.

Doubtless at first the chair was in itself simple enough, and it has grown to its present dignity of form and circumstance by gradual and natural stages, just as the useful crutch has become the symbolic crozier. But what the first thrones lacked in splendour of design, they gained in dignity of position. In the days of Basilican churches the altar stood on the chord of the arc formed by the apse, and the stalls of the clergy were ranged in a semi-circle behind it, with the bishop's chair on a dais in the midst. Thence, with his clergy on either hand, and looking over the altar at the congregation assembled in the nave, the bishop preached to, and blessed, his people.

This arrangement of the church is referred to, among other early writers, by St. Gregory Nazianzen, who describes himself sitting as bishop on the high throne, with the priests on lower benches ; the Apostolical Constitutions also allude to the same thing.   Even on the continent, where churches of the basilican type are still found, another order now prevails, yet at Nantes an almost perfect example exists, although the apsidal east-end of the cathedral is as late as the eleventh century in date ; while further south in France, the ancient arrangement may not infrequently be seen, save that some decorative feature, such as a pair of folding doors, has usurped the original place of the throne.

Over the elevated seat thus set apart for the " Father of the Diocese " a handsome covering was thrown, characteristic either by its richness or its decoration of its purpose.   St. Athanasius, in one of his apologies, speaks of a " Throne episcopally draped ; " and St. Augustine of Hippo, warns Maximin, the Donatist Bishop, that " neither thrones raised on steps, nor covered (perhaps canopied) seats," will avail one at the Last Judgment.

At the same time the Church was jealous of too much display in the state of the episcopate. At the Council of Antioch (A.D. 341) one of the charges against Paul of Samosata was that he had built himself a lofty tribune, too much resembling those of secular princes. It was the Church's care, in the quaint words of Bingham, that "the honours bestowed on her bishops should be such as might set them above contempt, but keep them below envy; make them venerable, but not minister to vanity." A practice similar to this of draping the throne with handsome stuffs, prevailed at old St. Paul's Cathedral, among the ornaments appertaining to which, in the seventh year of Edward VI., were "baudkins of divers sorts and colours, for garnishing the quire for the King's coming, and for the Bishop's seat."

With a different style of architecture, a different arrangement of the seats for the clergy became necessary; and in England, at any rate, where basilican churches were probably never common, the usual position seems always to have been on the south side of the choir, between the altar and the 'canons' stalls, although the marble chair, known as St. Augustine's chair, at Canterbury, is said at one time to have stood behind the altar, after the ancient style.

Some of the earliest representations of episcopal thrones occur on coins, especially on those of the Italian cities, which, in the days when they were separate republics, generally marked their money with the figures of their patron saints. A coin of Milan bears on its obverse the effigy of St. Ambrose, in full episcopal vestments, his right hand raised in benediction; he sits on a square seat, without arms or back, but carved in front, and having an embroidered cushion upon it. Other examples exhibit thrones almost equally simple, though various in shape. Several of the English Archbishops, both of Canterbury and York, issued a coinage of silver pennies, previous to the Norman Conquest; but, though they stamped them with their own names, and sometimes with an exceedingly rough representation of their faces, English art at that time was evidently unequal to the task of attempting the delineation of the whole figure.

For primitive English examples we may turn to the illuminated manuscripts of our monkish scribes. One of the Royal manuscripts has a figure of St. Augustine seated in a carved chair, the arms of which terminate in the heads of animals, and the feet of which are correspondingly clawed ; the seat is cushioned, and the whole is elevated on a shallow step, or dais. A Harleian manuscript has a figure of the same saint, enthroned on a chair precisely similar, which would imply that the seat in question was drawn from one actually in use, unless the artists copied one from the other.

An ancient episcopal chair is preserved at Hereford. It is a substantial seat with spindles in the arms, and in front and sides below the seat. But this was probably never the official throne of the See. It was usual for a movable chair to be provided, wherein the bishop might sit in any part of the cathedral in which he might be ministering. This was often made to fold up, for convenience of carriage, and was conse-quently termed *faldistorium ;* and although the Hereford chair is not of that type, it was doubtless used in a similar way.

Several of the early English thrones were of stone, which, by its very solidity and durability, gave them, however simple in form, a restrained dignity.   Allusion has already been made to St. Augustine's chair at Canterbury ; another example is the " Frithstool," or " seat of peace " in Hexham Abbey.   At the time of the abolition of the right of sanctuary, this had been long used as the spot to be gained by the fugitive criminal ere he could claim the church's protection ; but it is scarcely questionable that originally it was the throne of the ancient see of Hexham, which existed from A.D. 681 to 825.   The throne used by the Bishops of Durham when presiding in the chapter-house belongs to the same class.

The fourteenth century was apparently a great time for the erection of thrones in the English cathedrals.   One of the most splendid in the country is at Exeter, the canopy of which, with its towering pinnacles soars almost to the roof.   The rearing of it was probably the work of Bishop Walter Stapledon (1308-1327), a great builder at Exeter, though by some it is ascribed to Bishop John Boothe (1465-1478).   Bishop Hatfield, of Durham (1345-1382) endowed his cathedral with a magnificent episcopal throne.   Below he prepared for his own entombment, and above, supported by arches of stone and reached by an equally solid stair, he placed the throne, thus to teach himself, it is said, to remember the dignity of the episcopate, and the frail mortality of the bishop. The throne at Lincoln was put up under the auspices of John de Welbourn, the minster treasurer, in the same century ; and those at Hereford, and several other cathedrals, are of about the same date. Thomas de Bekinton, bishop of Bath and Wells from 1443 to 1466, is credited with the throne at Wells, but many consider it an earlier work. At Chester, fragments of the shrine of the abbess-patroness St. Werburga, destroyed at the Reformation, have been built up into a throne.

The most modern English episcopal throne is that in Norwich Cathedral, a handsome and dignified structure, which was erected in 1895 to commemorate the episcopate of nearly forty years of Bishop Pelham (1857-1893).

Many of our cathedrals were also abbey-churches, and in these the bishop had a dual office. He was both bishop of the diocese and abbot of the monastery, the dean being his prior. Thus it happens that at Durham, Carlisle, Ely, and elsewhere, the bishop had assigned to him not only his throne, but also the first stall on the south side (the abbot's stall), the dean in these cases having the opposite one.

Chantries.

By John T. Page.

"He sette not his benefice to hire,
And lette his shepe accombred in the mire;
And run into London unto Seint Pouls,
To seken him a chanterie for soules."

—Chaucer.

THE equivalent of the word chantry in mediæval Latin was *Cantaria*, which in French is expressed as *Chanterie* from *Chanter*, to sing.

Chantries may be said to have flourished in England, roughly speaking, from the fourteenth to the middle of the sixteenth century. Most of the churches which date back to this period still retain traces of chantries within their walls. These were established in nearly every parish, and could literally be counted by the thousand at the time when the fiat went forth for their suppression. During the Middle Ages the belief in purgatory was real and widespread. The clergy pourtrayed with harrowing details the torments of lost souls, and enhanced their descriptions by the aid of startling frescoes on the church walls. Thus it came about that those who possessed money were easily persuaded to set apart a portion of it in order that prayer might continually be made for the repose of their souls. For this purpose small private chapels were either added to or divided from the parish churches by those who could afford to do so. Here priests were employed to keep up a perpetual succession of prayers for the prosperity of the founder and his family while they lived, and for the repose of their souls when they died. Within the precincts of the chapel their bodies were eventually committed to the dust, and richly sculptured altar tombs were erected over their remains. Many of these gorgeous memorials still exist, although the small enclosures in which they were enshrined have long ago been demolished.

Sometimes as many as half-a-dozen chantries were attached to an ordinary parish church, and in St. Paul's Cathedral, at the suppression, there were found to be no fewer than forty-seven such foundations within its walls.

The service in the chantry was very simple. It was usually conducted by a priest and his acolyte, no congregation whatever being necessarily present.   Bishop Jewell, in condemning these "private masses," speaks of them as being "for the most part sayde inside iles alone, without companye of people, onely with one boye to make answer."

In constructing a chantry, it was customary to enclose a part of either the north or south aisle of the church at the east end.   The partitions were composed of stone-work or wood, the bottom part being panelled and the upper part open-work like the rood screen dividing the chancel from the nave of the church.   Most of these partitions have now entirely disappeared, but in some cases they are intact.   A piscina in the outer wall of the edifice is often the only remaining indication of the position of a chantry.   It should here be mentioned that chantries were not always contiguous to a church.   In some cases buildings were specially erected for this purpose near the residence of the founder.

A few examples of the stone altars at which mass was said in the chantries still exist.   A very good specimen of one of these may be seen at Warmington Church, Warwickshire.   It consists of a slab of stone marked with crosses at each angle and in the centre. It is let into the wall and supported from beneath on three stone brackets. The founder's tomb was occasionally utilised as an altar, but this was not often the case.

The Beauchamp Chapel attached to St. Mary's Church, Warwick, may be cited as one of the finest chantries now to be seen in England. Under directions contained in the will of Richard Beauchamp, Earl of Warwick, it was commenced in 1443, and is constructed in the purest Gothic style. It took twenty-one years to accomplish its completion, the cost, including the elaborate altar-tomb of the founder, being £2,481, equal to about £40,000 in the present day. It is, practically speaking, still intact, and contains many choicely sculptured tombs and memorials. Another very good specimen is to be seen at the little village of Kirk Sandall, in Yorkshire. It was founded by William Rokeby, Archbishop of Dublin, who died in 1521. He was a native of the place, and left directions in his will that his body should be buried at Kirk Sandall, his heart at Halifax, and his bowels at Dublin.

During the time that chantries were in vogue, they were frequently established by royal personages. In such cases much money was spent on their internal decoration, and they were, of course, very richly endowed. A royal chantry formerly existed on the spot now occupied by the north aisle of the Church of All Hallows, Barking, in the city of London. It was founded by King Richard I., and dedicated to the Virgin Mary. Some even believe that the "lion heart" of Richard was buried here, but this is, to say the least, very doubtful. As a royal foundation, established for the benefit of King Richard and his successors, great care was naturally bestowed upon it by later kings of England, notably by Edward I., Edward IV., and Richard III. Many allusions to this chantry occur in old documents. The following entries are from the "Privy purse expenses of Elizabeth of York" (1470).

> Paid to our Ladye of Berkinge xi[s.] vi[d.]
> Item to Sr. William Barton, preest, singinge
> at oure Ladye of Barkinge vi[s.] viii[d.]

Another celebrated royal chantry is that of Henry V., at Westminster Abbey, which occupies the whole of the east end of the chapel of Edward the Confessor. Some of the grandest sculpture in the venerable edifice is to be seen in this chapel.

The commencement of the crusade against chantries, which ultimately led to their dissolution, may be traced to the year 1529, when an Act was passed forbidding any person to receive money for celebrating Mass for the souls of the dead. This Act effectually prevented the establishment of any new foundations, but did not affect those already in existence. In 1545, a statute provided that the revenues of the chantries should be temporarily appropriated for the King's use, but this only lasted until Henry's death. A more drastic measure was then set on foot. Soon after the first parliament of the young king, Edward VI., met, an Act was passed (1 Ed. VI., c. 14) which permanently dissolved all chantries and confiscated all their endowments. The avowed object of its promoters was to convert the foundations into " good and godly uses, in erecting grammar schools, in farther augmenting the universities, and making better provision for the poor and needy." *

That nothing of the kind was intended, the sequel amply proved. This was, indeed, " a harvest time for thieves, and a high holiday for the profane." † It is true that a few grammar schools

* Collier.   † Lane.

—still known as King Edward the Sixth's schools
—·were established throughout the country, and
the hospitals of St. Bartholomew and St. Thomas
were provided with endowments for the relief of
the sick poor ; but the bulk of the spoil was used
to defray the warlike operations in Scotland and
Ireland, and last, but not least, to enrich the
coffers of the court sycophants.   " Educational
endowments had to be left for later reigns, and
largely to private munificence. The unique
opportunity which the dissolution of the chantries
presented for advancing the cause of education
was practically lost." *

The uses to which the chantry chapels had been
put amounted to a parody on religion, and the cry
for reformation was irresistible and imperative.
But the change proved too sudden to be useful.
Things once held in reverence became common
and profane, and money bequeathed for pious uses
was squandered like water to compass the ends of
unscrupulous courtiers.   Thus the remedy was in
many respects worse than the disease.

The chantries desecrated and demolished, their
revenues misappropriated and misspent, and their
priests turned adrift to face a frowning world—

* William Page, F.S.A.

such is the picture of havoc that meets our gaze as we turn back to the stirring period of the Reformation. In these later times, all that is left to us is a mass of beautiful wreckage, which the hand of demolition has scattered along the shores of time.

Hagioscopes.

By John T. Page.

A HAGIOSCOPE, or Squint, generally consists of an oblique opening in the interior walls of a church, cut through the angle formed by the junction of the north or south aisles with the chancel. It is carried through the thickness of the wall immediately at the back of the pillar which supports the chancel arch. By this means a good view is obtained of the east end of the chancel, which would otherwise be quite hidden from anyone occupying a position at the eastern ends of the aisles. It will at once be obvious that during the time when the Chantries or private chapels were in vogue, something of the kind was necessary in order that the elevation of the host, and other ceremonies conducted at the high altar, might be witnessed and participated in by the Chantry priests. Examples of these oblique openings, or hagioscopes, are to be found in nearly every county in England, but, notwithstanding this, they are by no means common.

It should here be mentioned that there are a few instances in which the sight line of a hagioscope is not directed towards the high altar, but to some other part of the building. As an example the church at Eastbourne may be cited, where the opening in the south pier of the chancel is directed towards the south aisle. This is, however, most unusual, and it is assumed that in such a case, the opening was made to overlook the tomb of the founder of a Chantry, where Mass was celebrated daily. This would enable any one to participate in the ceremony, without of necessity entering the private chapel.

Sometimes the openings are continued in a line through more than one wall, as in Bridgwater Church, Somerset, where an opening, now bricked up, in the north porch, commands a hagioscope in the north transept, through which the position occupied by the high altar may be viewed.

At Tilebrook Church, Bedfordshire, the north aisle is continued eastward, so as to form a chapel, which contains a hagioscope and a piscina combined, and at Minster Lovell Church, Oxfordshire, there is a hagioscope in each transept, and another opening from the vestry.

Most of these hagioscopes are perfectly plain

slits in the masonry, and are quite devoid of ornament, as at Stepney Church, Middlesex, but there are very occasionally to be seen specimens of a more ornate description. At Hadleigh Church, Essex, there are openings both in the north and south piers of the chancel arch, which are cinque-foiled in shape, and at Irthling-borough Church, Northamptonshire, the head of the opening is arched, cinque-foiled within, and surmounted by an embattled moulding.

In modern times many of these hagioscopes have been glazed at both ends, and thus temporarily closed, and in some cases, they have been permanently blocked up with masonry.

Where they still exist, they generally serve the purpose of silent witnesses against a system of architecture which has not yet succeeded in devising a scheme whereby every worshipper can see and participate in the most important part of the services of the church.

Some English Shrines.

BY THE REV. GEO. S. TYACK, B.A.

WHILE not questioning the fact that good was wrought by that great upheaval which is commonly called the Reformation, it is impossible for the thinking man to close his eyes to the excesses to which its leaders drifted, both in thought and deed. It is not the province of a volume such as this to discuss the strictly religious results of that stormy time, but the artist and the antiquary can hardly deplore too deeply the havoc which it wrought in the domains most interesting to them during the century or more that elapsed between the beginning of the Reformation and the end of the Commonwealth. Nothing that was beautiful, nothing hallowed by the veneration of the ages, seems to have been able to touch a tender chord in the spoilers' souls ; and if much that is both lovely and venerable has nevertheless been spared to us, it is chiefly owing to good fortune, or to the happy skill of our ancestors in combining artistic beauty with almost impreg-

nable strength.   Thus, while our massive cathedrals remain to us, and our once glorious abbeys,
though disused as well as desecrated, still, after
three centuries of neglect, rear many a sightless
window and graceful tower to defy the winds, —
the painted glass all aglow with inimitable colour,
the statues of saints and martyrs, and the tombs
and shrines of the great and the holy of old time,
these have been grievously mutilated, or swept
totally away.

The mediæval Church loved to show her devotion to the saintly dead by the erection of shrines
in their honour.   Some of the most ornate
portions of our cathedrals were built specially to
receive them, and on the shrines themselves all
the resources of art were willingly lavished.

The shrine of St. Thomas à Becket at Canterbury needs only to be mentioned in illustration.
It was, we are told, " blazing with gold and
jewels, and embossed with innumerable pearls
and jewels and rings."   But even this is reported
to have been surpassed in magnificence by the
tomb of St. Cuthbert of Durham, "of costly
green marble, all limned and gilt with gold."

Almost all our cathedrals contained the bones
of some local saint, whose last resting-place

devotion and patriotism combined to honour and
adorn.   Thus York cherished in its minster the
relics of St. William, archbishop (with an
interval), from 1143 to 1154; Lincoln, those of
St. Hugh, bishop from 1186 to 1203; and Hereford, those of St. Thomas (Thomas de Cantelupe),
whose arms still form the armorial bearings of the
see, bishop from 1275 to 1283.   Oxford, Ely,
and Chester boasted the possession respectively
of the abbesses, St. Frideswide (died 735), St.
Etheldreda (died 697), and St. Werburgh (died
699).   St. Wulfstan (1002-1016) reposed in his
cathedral at Worcester, St. Wilfrid (664-709) at
Ripon, St. Richard (1245-1253) at Chichester,
St. David (died 544) at St. David's, St. Swithun
(852-862) at Winchester, St. Osmond (1078-
1099) at Salisbury, and St. Paulinus, the com-
panion of St. Augustine (633-644), at Rochester,
all bishops of the sees in which they were afterwards venerated.   Rochester also raised a shrine
for St. William of Perth; and of the English
kings, St. Oswald, the martyred sovereign of
Northumbria, was honoured at Worcester, and
St. Edward the Confessor at Westminster; while
at Gloucester the unhappy Edward II. was
esteemed a saint and a martyr, and his body was

preserved in a richly-carved shrine, which still
exists. Of all these, and of the many shrines of
minor interest, once standing in the cathedrals
and the great abbey churches of England, few
now remain ; and even the sacred contents of
most have disappeared. The shrine of the Confessor, of course, is still to be seen at Westminster ; the lower part, consisting of the actual
tomb of St. Thomas, is found at Hereford, and
portions of the shrine of St. Frideswide yet exist
at Oxford ; while the various fragments of that of
St. Alban have recently been discovered and
laboriously pieced together. Of several others
the bases alone remain, and in some few cases the
bodies were undisturbed at the destruction of
their shrines, or were re-interred after it.
Durham still boasts the relics of St. Cuthbert ;
Salisbury, those of St. Osmond ; Canterbury,
those of St. Alphege ; and Ripon perhaps those
of St. Wilfrid.

The history of these sacred repositories is very
similar in outline. It will be useful to follow in
some detail the fortunes of one, as an example of
all ; and for this purpose we turn to the shrine of
St. Hugh of Lincoln, as being in its time one of
the most famous in the country, yet to us of

to-day not so well known as those of St. Thomas of Canterbury or St. Edward the Confessor.

Hugh of Avalon, afterwards to be venerated as St. Hugh of Lincoln, came to the throne of that see in 1186, and after a reign of seventeen years, during which his gentle firmness and un-flinching devotion to duty commanded both the affection and respect of his contemporaries, from the graceless King John to the meanest of his people, he died in London in 1203. The body, brought with all pious care to his cathedral city, was buried in the chapel of St. John Baptist, near the cloister door.

The name and fame of Hugh soon brought such multitudes of devotees to visit his tomb, in hope of some signal blessing for soul or body through the intercession of so holy a man, that the little chapel proved all too small for their convenience. The walls were therefore carried out some fifty feet further in length, and, at the same time, the relics were translated to a more dignified tomb in the centre of the chapel.

St. Hugh was formally canonized in 1220, and from that time increased efforts were made to pro-vide for his remains a resting-place commensurate with the esteem in which they were held. In

1256, a scheme far more ambitious than the mere enlargement of a side chapel was begun. The apse terminating the choir of the cathedral was pulled down, and a new and noble addition was commenced. This extension, known as the angel choir, provided a worthy site for a splendid shrine, and ample room for the many pilgrims. This building was not itself complete, when, on October 6th, 1280, the second and final translation of St. Hugh's relics took place amid a scene of pomp probably never equalled in Lincoln.

It was usual, in erecting a shrine, to place it immediately behind the reredos of the high altar, and to so raise it as to make it visible to the priest while saying Mass, the object being to raise his thoughts, with his eyes, to the example of the saint whose tomb stood before him. So was placed the shrine of St. Cuthbert, at Durham; so, too, that of St. William, at York, and many others; and so, too, probably stood the shrine of St. Hugh, at Lincoln.

The custom in Wales was an exception to this rule, the favourite position being on the side of the choir. St. David's shrine was on the north side in his cathedral, and that of St. Teilo on the south side at Llandaff.

At Lincoln, on a lofty stone base was placed a
metal " bere " or portable shrine, adorned with
jewels and the precious metals ; a grill of curiously
wrought ironwork was added later to protect it,
and a cover, inlaid with gold and silver figures,
surmounted all.   Plates of beaten gold covered
the tomb, which was eight feet long and four feet
broad.

Although the body was thus removed to the
angel choir, the chapel of St. John Baptist was
not shorn entirely of its glories, for the head of St.
Hugh was replaced in it, and was presently provided with a gold reliquary of its own, beautifully
enamelled and jewelled.   A mitre of silver gilt
accompanied   the   head,   and   rings   set   with
sapphires, beryls, and other stones, together with
old gold coins and branches of coral, adorned
either   the   sacred   relic   itself,   or   its   case.   A
chained copy of the life of St. Hugh stood somewhere near for the instruction of the visitors.

It was a usual thing for a church, having more
than one relic of a saint, or relics that had become
separated into parts, to distribute them in different
chapels in this way.   At Chichester, the body, the
head, and the chalice of St. Richard had each its
proper place.   At York, too, and at Lichfield, the

heads and bodies of St. William and of St. Chad were severally provided for.

When so much treasure was lavished upon relics, it will be obvious that great care had need to be shown in guarding them. We are not surprised, therefore, at finding quite a retinue of keepers of various degrees employed about the shrine. These consisted of two principal keepers, with a day-keeper and two night-keepers, all of whom had assistants. Besides these there was a chaplain, with deacon, sub-deacon, and choristers.

Alms-boxes stood near the shrine, into which the faithful pilgrims dropt their thank-offerings, and the record of the opening of these twice yearly—at Whitsuntide, and at the feast of the translation of St. Hugh (October 7th)—has come down to us fairly complete from 1339 to 1532. The largest amount noted is £37 14s. 8d. in 1365. In the fifteenth century it begins to show a perceptible decline, and in the sixteenth it reaches only five or six pounds a year.

From the money thus collected wax was purchased, presumably for tapers to burn at the shrine ; and the residue was divided amongst the cathedral officials, clerical and lay, in sums varying from 20s. for the actual guardians of the shrine, to 3d. each for the sacristy-clerk and the clerk of the fabric, and 18d. to be divided amongst the boys of the choir. Those employed about the tomb had a special allowance from the fund for wine.

It was not always, nor even frequently, that the offerings at a shrine were thus distributed. More commonly the fabric of the church, or some other more general object, benefitted by the gifts of the faithful. The alms-box at the shrine of St. William of Perth, at Rochester, provided means for erecting the east end of the cathedal ; and pilgrims to the resting-place of St. Wilfrid gave no small help towards building the cathedral at Ripon.

It is not, perhaps, a difficult matter for an age which has lost all faith in saints, and almost all in the possibility of saintliness, to find ground for scornful derision in the devotion of the men of old, to the tombs of the hallowed dead ; but it is, at least, open to question, whether such a method of raising funds for religious purposes was not quite as legitimate and consistent as the modern fancy for the frivolity of a " Bazaar," or the feebleness of an amateur concert.

In spite of all the guardians and clerks who

watched the relics of St. Hugh, a sacrilegious theft
of the head was perpetrated in 1364. Monastic
chronicles are not wanting in stories of monks
who, for the honour of their own house, have
" conveyed" thither venerated relics found in the
churches of their neighbours ; but in this case it
was not the head of the saint, but the casket
containing it, that formed the temptation. A
speedy vengeance, however, dogged the sinners'
steps. Their ill-got wealth was in turn stolen
from them, and they were arrested, convicted,
and hanged ; while the head, miraculously preserved from harm, tradition tells, came into the
hands of the king, Edward III., who restored it
to Lincoln.

The next robbery of the shrine was more
successful, as it was more thorough. Along with
most other churches, containing anything of
value, Lincoln Minster was plundered by royal
warrant at the Reformation, and the shrine with
all its gold and jewels, vanished. Far into the
eighteenth century, the iron clamps which secured
some portion of it to the ground, remained to
mark the spot, but even those have now disappeared. The body was long supposed to have
been re-buried in a grave within the retro-choir,

and Bishop Fuller (1667-1675) erected a tomb
over the spot ; but recent investigation has shown
that if indeed the relics of St. Hugh were ever
laid there, they were again removed, let us hope
by pious hands.

Besides the splendid shrine of which we have
been speaking, Lincoln Cathedral had others of
less note. The body of St. John of Dalderby,
bishop from 1300 to 1320, lay in a shrine of
silver, and another was erected over the remains
of "little St. Hugh," the Christian child, said to
have been crucified by the Lincoln Jews. So, in
Ely also, three other holy abbesses shared the
honours of St. Ethelburga ; at Durham, the
Venerable Bede kept watch over the western
chapel, as did St. Cuthbert over the eastern one,
while Canterbury had the shrines of several
saintly archbishops, and others.

For the better guardianship of these hallowed
spots, a special chamber was often erected for the
caretakers. Those at St. Alban's, a handsome
structure of two storeys, and at Oxford yet
remain. In other cases with the need of the
watch the watching-chamber has gone.

Alas ! that in speaking of the English shrines,
one should have to speak always of what has been,

or of the fragments, the shadows, the dry records only, that remain to us. If the veneration of centuries, if the glories of art, had no voice that could be heard against the clamorous cupidity of the despoiler, surely one might have hoped that the presence of the holy dead would have availed to arrest the royal tyrant and the puritan bigot in their career of sacrilege and crime.

The Church and Well of St. Chad.

By J. A. Langford, ll.d.

A SHORT but pleasant walk from Lichfield Cathedral, by the side of Stowe Pool, leads to the ancient and famous Church and Well of St. Chad. Both in history and legend they are indissolubly united, and the church cannot be mentioned without the well being recalled at the same time. Their history is an important chapter in the Church History of Staffordshire, and is a very interesting record to all lovers of antiquity, and who take a pride in tracing the course of their country's progress and the life of her people. The Church of St. Chad is the oldest, and in some respects the most interesting, foundation in Lichfield—older than the Cathedral which, since its formation to the present time, is, of course, one of the most important, as it is one of the most beautiful, buildings in the country. But the cathedral is the outcome and owes its existence to the little cell of the saint on the site of which is the present church. Authorities differ somewhat as to the

13

exact dates, but the most generally received belief is that the church goes back to 669, while the cathedral was founded in 700 A.D.

The Venerable Bede gives a full account of St. Chad in his " Ecclesiastical History." This has been well summarised, so far as our subject is concerned, by the Rev. T. Harwood, in his History of Lichfield :—" In 669, St. Ceaddn, Ceddn, or Chad, succeeded to the episcopal seat in this place. He first retired to Lichfield for the purpose of religious solitude, where he led (as legend tells us), an eremitical life in a cell, by the side of a spring, near the place upon which the church of his name now stands, and supported himself upon the milk of a doe. Here, attended by Ovin and a few other pious men, he was accustomed to preach and pray. The spot thus chosen by St. Chad for his habitation was well adapted to inspire sentiments of devotion. It was in the midst of a wood, and a little river ran by the side of it. The church was small, according to the age in which it was erected, and here St. Chad was buried." Then he quotes from Dr. Stukeley, who wrote in 1756, " I have long ago taken drawings of St. Chad's habitation, by the neighbouring church of Lichfield, where Ovin heard the angels at St.

Chad's obituary.   There is his well, and a little monastery ; the habitation joins on the north-west angle of the church."   Leland, who visited Lichfield about 1538, thus refers to the church and well in his Itinerary :—" Stowe Church, in the easte end of the towne, where is St. Chad's well —a spring of pure water, where is seen a stone at the bottom of it—on the whiche, some say, St. Chadd was wont naked to stande in the water and praye.   At this stone St. Chad had his oratory in the tyme Wulphar, King of the Merches."

In these early times, when England was being converted to Christianity, preachers like St. Chad always selected for their cells and habitations places near to a stream, a spring, or a well, water being necessary for the ceremony of baptism. The natural consequences followed.   Immediately after, and often before, the death of the holy man, miraculous power was ascribed to the waters of the stream, or spring, or well.   This was especially the case with wells, as a large number of holy wells in the county remain to testify.   Hence arose Well Worship, which was accompanied with religious ceremonies, some of them very beautiful, some quite innocent, and others neither beautiful nor innocent.   In addition to these ceremonies, each well was visited by large numbers of pilgrims, especially by persons suffering from any kind of disease, who sought relief and health by drinking, or washing themselves in the miraculous waters, whose health-bestowing efficacy was never doubted. This well worship was never approved by the church, and was "strictly prohibited by the Anglican councils," even in the earliest times. These prohibitions had little effect, and were generally, if not universally, disregarded, so strong is the power of custom when united with religious or with any superstitious belief.

During the Puritan rule all such observances, ceremonies, and customs were rigidly suppressed. At the Restoration, however, the people returned to their old use and wont; and although pilgrimages had ceased, and the religious sentiment which formerly accompanied these observances had very little influence, the custom of adorning, and having processions in honour of the well, was made the occasion for a general holiday. In Staffordshire the day selected for this purpose was Holy Thursday. In his natural history of the county, Dr. Plot says: "They have a custom in this county of adorning their wells on Holy

Thursday with boughs and flowers. This, it seems, they do in all gospel places, whether wells, trees, or hills, which, being now observed only for decency and custom sake, is innocent enough. Heretofore it was usual to pay this respect to such wells as were eminent for curing distempers on the saint's day whose name the well bore; diverting themselves with cakes and ale, and a little music and dancing, which, whilst within these bounds, was also an innocent recreation." Most readers will recall the lines in "Comus," in which Milton sings the old honours paid' to the Severn :—

> " The shepherds at these festivals
> Carol her good deeds in rustic lays,
> And throw sweet garland wreaths into her stream
> Of pansies, pinks, and gaudy daffodils."

The custom was carried out at St. Chad's Well in the olden time with much ceremony. From various sources, from bits taken from one writer and bits from another, we are enabled to form a rather clear idea, and to present a rather complete picture of this now curious old Church custom. Early on the morning of Holy Thursday, the citizens would be busily employed in dressing the well to make it beautiful for the coming festival. This was done by decorating it with wreaths and garlands of freshly-gathered flowers, interspersed with slips from shrubs and branches from the newly-budding trees. The flowers were arranged in such devices as the fancy or taste of the men and women engaged in the work suggested. Here differently-shaped boards were used, which were covered with moist clay in which they placed the stems of the flowers arranged in diverse patterns, which it is stated made a very beautiful sight, the damp clay, of course, preserving their freshness. These were so suspended about the well that the flowing water seemed to come between beds of flowers. This labour of love finished, the workers put on their holiday clothes ready for the next part of the day's proceedings.

In olden times a service was held in the church ; after which the people, with all the children arrayed in their Sunday best, and carrying flowers, formed in procession, and marched to the well. Then the clergyman read the psalms, epistle, and gospel for the day ; and this portion of the festival was concluded by the church choir and people singing a hymn ; the singing was accompanied by music. The remainder of the

day was spent in rustic sports, in dancing, and
in other harmless and innocent modes of recreation.
In this manner a religious ceremony was combined with secular festivity.   Similar observances,
with local variations, were observed at nearly all
holy wells; but the midland counties were
especially distinguished by the number of such
places, and by the thoroughness with which the
people celebrated the day.

The ceremony is still observed at St. Chad's
Well, but it is sadly shorn of its ancient glory,
and robbed of its ancient significance.   Writing
early in the present century, the Rev. Mr.
Nightingale says, "Even at this day, it is customary for the clergyman and churchwardens, and
a great concourse of children, to visit this well on
Holy Thursday (Ascension 'Day), when it is
adorned with boughs and flowers, and the gospel
for the day is read."   This description, with slight
alterations, will fairly describe the ceremony at
present performed.   On Holy Thursday, the
choristers of the cathedral "walk in procession to
the well, carrying green boughs, and sing the
old 100th Psalm, and the Priest Vicar reads the
Holy Gospel for that day."

The holiday, the procession, the loving labour of

decorating the well, and the festivities, the sports, and the general rejoicings of the olden time have ceased and passed away, never likely to be again restored. It is useless to preserve a form, when the spirit which gave it vitality is dead. Still we are pleased that even this rather poor survival of an old custom remains, to call attention to the things which delighted and made glad the hearts of our forefathers, in the dim and distant past. Such reflections are not without their happy effects on the minds in which they arise. It is a pity to lose any of the old customs which added to the harmless pleasures of life, and gave a touch of poetry to the otherwise prosaic intercourse of daily existence. At such times, when thus recalling the days that are no more, and for a little time living in the past, we sympathize with nature's great poet, and exclaim with Wordsworth :—

> " Would that our scrupulous sires had dared to leave
>   Less scanty measure of those graceful rites
>   And usages, whose due return invites
>   A stir of mind too natural to deceive ;
>   Giving to Memory help when she would weave
>   A crown for Hope ! "

Burials in Woollen.

By WILLIAM ANDREWS, F.R.H.S.

A SINGULAR sumptuary law was passed in 1666 to enforce burials in woollen. The Act was devised by Parliament professedly for the encouragement of woollen manufactures, and prevention of the exportation of moneys for the buying and importing linen. It is to be feared that it was really the outcome of a selfish spirit of protection, similar to that shewn in the Act which prohibited the importation of cattle bred in Ireland and fish caught by foreigners.

After March 25th, 1667, the Act directed that no person should " be buried in any shirt, or sheet, other than should be made of wooll onely." The Act even prohibited the use of linen for quilling round the inside of the coffin, and the ligature round the feet of the corpse ; both were to be of woollen. A custom which was more ancient than Christianity was hard to put aside. The practice of wrapping the dead in linen is of great antiquity. It is not surprising to learn that the

Act was almost a dead letter. The fines were seldom enforced, for reliable information could not be easily obtained, and could only as a rule be given by the parties most interested in concealing the transgression.

A more stringent Act was passed in 1678. The first Act consisted of two clauses only, and the second Act recites these, and includes a number of clauses. The Act says that it is intended for the "lessening the importation of linen from beyond the seas and the encouragement of the woollen and paper manufacturers of this kingdom."

In the second section of this Act it is stated " Noe Corpse of any person or persons shall be buried in any Shirt, Shift, Sheete, or Shroud, or any thing whatsoever made or mingled with Flax, Hempe, Silke, Haire, Gold or Silver, or any stuffe or thing other than what is made of Sheep's Wooll onely, or be put in any coffin lined or faced with any sort of Cloath or Stuffe or any thing whatsoever that is made of any Materiall but Sheep's Wooll onely, upon paine of the forfeiture of five pounds of lawfull money of England," etc.

Another section enacted that the clergy were to keep a register of burials, and in it to record affidavits that had previously been made before a justice of peace for the county, or other person authorised by the Act.

When the Act was broken, half the penalty went to the poor of the parish and the other half to the informer. Usually, by arrangement, a servant of the household, or someone whom the family desired to receive the benefit, laid information.

The Act provided that persons dying of the plague might be buried without a penalty being incurred, even if linen were used.

In section nine it was directed that "this Act shall be publiquely read upon the first Sunday after the Feast of St. Bartholomew every yeare for seaven yeares next following, presently after Divine Service."

Dr. T. N. Brushfield, in his paper on "The Church of All Saints, East Budleigh," read at a meeting of the Devonshire Association for the Advancement of Science, Literature, and Art, at Plymouth, July, 1892, has an interesting note on burials in woollen. "The earliest allusion to this subject at East Budleigh," writes Dr. Brushfield, "in our parish accounts are as follow :—

1678-9. For Act for Buring in Wooling ...	co oo o8	
For a Register Book for Burying		
in Woollen	oo o1 oo"	

Copies of the Register were sent to the Sessions, *e.g.* :—

"1688-9.   p^d for a transcript for ye burying
            in woollen only w^{cb} was putt
            in att the Sessions   ...   ... oo oi oo
 1689-90. p^d for a transcript for those
            buried in woollen   ...   ... oo oi oo"

At the conclusion of the burial service it was customary for the parish clerk to call out, " Who makes the affidavit ? " A chief relation came forward and took the necessary oath, and this was duly noted in the register.

The following is a common form of an affidavit :—

"*Elizabeth Bryant*, of the parish of *Radmill*, in the county of *Sussex*, maketh oath that Elizabeth Ford, of the parish of *Radmill*, in the county of *Sussex*, lately deceased, was not put in, wrapt up, or wound up, or buried in any shirt, shift, sheet, or shroud, made or mingled with flax, hemp, silk, hair, gold or silver, or any other than what is made of sheep's wool only ; nor in any coffin lined or faced with any cloth, stuff, or any other thing whatsoever made or mingled with flax, hemp, silk, hair, gold, or silver, or any other material contrary to the Act of Parliament for burying in woollen, but sheep's wool only. Dated the 16 day of *Jan.*, 1724."

It will not be without interest to show the manner of recording the affidavits in the parish books. The first is from Newburn-on-Tyne :—

"1687, 18 Aug. Cuthbert Longridge was buried in
woollen, as by a certificate dated 24 Aug., 1687."

An entry from Lamesley, county of Durham, is
to the effect :—

"1678. Anne Marley wrapped in sheep's skin, bur."

From Woolvercot, Oxon., is the following :—

"1693, August 17. Catherine, dau. of Sir William
Juxon, buried in woollen.—Affidavit."

Records of no affidavits are by no means uncommon, and we give as illustrations particulars
of two. The first is drawn from the register of
St. Mary-le-Bow, Durham :—

"Christopher Bell, Gent., was lapped in linen contrary
to the late Act, Dec., 1678."

The next example is from the Gainsborough,
Lincolnshire, burial register :—

"6th Sept., 1703. Buried Thomas Day Batchellor.
No Affidavit."

In 1730 was interred, in Westminster Abbey,
Mrs. Ann Oldfield, a celebrated actress. She
gave her maid, Mrs. Elizabeth Saunders, also a
clever actress, instructions respecting the manner
she desired to be dressed when dead. She
wished to wear "a very fine Brussels' lace head-
dress, a holland shift with a tucker, and double

ruffles of the same lace, and a pair of new kid gloves, and was then wrapped in a winding-sheet of linen." Pope, in his "Moral Essays," thus refers to Mrs. Oldfield :—

> "Odious! in woollen! 'twould a saint provoke,
> Were the last words that poor Narcessa spoke:
> No, let a charming chintz and Brussels' lace
> Wrap my cold limbs, and shade my lifeless face;
> One would not, sure, be frightful when one's dead:
> And, Betty, give the cheek a little red."

The parish book of St. John the Baptist, Chester, contains a quaint entry bearing on this subject well worth reproducing :—

> "1689. The Churchwardens paid, by request of Widow Gardener, to four poore widdows of her daughter's acquaintance, her daughter being buried in Linen, 02 10 00."

Some curious information is contained in a book published in London in 1719, under the title of "M. Misson's Memoirs and Observations in his Travels over England, etc., disposed in Alphabetical Order, written originally in French, and translated by Mr. Ozell." The work made its first appearance in 1698, and was published at the Hague. The manners and customs of our countrymen are fully noticed, and usually in an entertaining style. When Sir Henry Ellis was

preparing a new edition of Brand's "Popular
Antiquities," he frequently drew upon Misson's
Travels for information to illustrate his work.
We find in his volume a curious account of the
custom of burying in woollen. "There is an
Act of Parliament," says Misson, "which ordains
that the dead shall be buried in a woollen stuff which
is a kind of thin bays, which they call flannel;
nor is it lawful to use the least needleful of
thread or silk. (The intention of this Act is for
the encouragement of the woollen manufacture.)
This shift is always white; but there are different
sorts of it as to fineness, and consequently
different prices. To make these dresses is a
particular trade, and there are many that sell
nothing else." We are told that a man's shirt
"has commonly a sleeve purfled about the wrists,
and the slit of the shirt done in the same manner.
This should be at least half-a-foot longer than the
body, that the feet of the deceased may be
wrapped in it as in a bag. Upon the head they
put a cap, which they fasten with a very broad
chin-cloth, with gloves on the hands, and a cravat
round the neck, all of woollen. The women
have a kind of head-dress with a forehead cloth.
. . ." He also states "That the body may ly

the softer, some put a lay of bran about four inches thick at the bottom of the coffin. The coffin is sometimes very magnificent. The body is visited to see that it is buried in flannel, and that nothing is sewed with thread. They let it lye three or four days."

The law of burying in woollen was introduced into Ireland in 1733, but the Irish Government, it is recorded, seldom enforced it. The Act was not repealed in England until 1814, but long before that period it had fallen into disuse.

Ibearse :

HOW A WORD HAS CHANGED ITS MEANING.

BY EDWARD PEACOCK, F.S.A.

ALL serious students of our mother tongue owe a deep debt of gratitude to the late Archbishop Trench for directing attention to the fact that words are *things*, and have a history of their own. We do not, of course, mean to imply that he was the first person to make the discovery, or even to point it out to English readers. Not to mention the great continental scholars with whose labours on Latin and Greek we have at present no concern, there are traces, faint though they be, that Sir Thomas Browne, on this as on many other matters, held ideas in suspension in his mind, though they were never formulated, which have a strikingly modern aspect. We are, however, indebted to a fierce political partizan—John Horne Tooke—for first compelling Englishmen to give attention to the history of the words they use. His *Diversions of Purley*, to which Dr. Trench made such graceful reference in the pre-

14

face to his *Lectures on the Study of Words*, was it seems the first work which attracted notice to a class of facts which had hitherto been almost completely neglected. It appeared upwards of fifty years before the Archbishop's book saw the light, during the crash and turmoil of the French Revolution (1798-1805), a time most unpropitious for thoughtful literature. Abounding as it does, not only in shortcomings, but in absolute errors, the Archbishop was unquestionably correct in saying, at the time he wrote, though it would be very far from being the case now, that his first acquaintance with that remarkable book had been " an epoch in many a student's intellectual life."

Another forerunner of the philology of our own day must not be passed by without some mention. Walter Whiter was a learned man, by no means without intellectual power ; but he held radically wrong notions regarding those great laws or forces which lie at the foundation of all rational speech. His *Etymologicon Universale, or Universal Etymological Dictionary* (1811-1825), was not only dipped into but widely read, and the very absurdity of some of the author's assumptions stimulated thought. Still, when all

this has been allowed for, we cannot but acknowledge that much of the earnest spirit of enquiry
regarding not only the words of our own
literary language, but also of the folk-speech
which still, we are happy to say, flourishes everywhere around us, is due to the memorable lectures
delivered by Trench to the pupils of Winchester
Training School, some forty-four years ago. The
New English Dictionary, which some of us think
the greatest literary work of the Victorian era, has
resulted from the combination of many causes, but
there cannot be a question that many of the
workers who have served and are serving under
the leadership of Dr. Murray, received their
first impulse towards a study of words from the
writing of Dr. Trench.

That the *New English Dictionary* is an immense advance on all that has gone before it,
is admitted by everyone; we doubt, however,
whether the historical treatment words receive
therein is generally appreciated as it deserves.
To us this is by far the most important part of
the work. It has, however, been found impossible to treat even the most important words with
the fulness that they deserve, when looked upon
as units in the great structure of English speech.

As time goes on we do not doubt that many of the words calendared in Dr. Murray's great work will be dealt with separately. We propose, so far as space will allow, to do so with one familiar term. It is no fitter for our purpose than hundreds of others which might have been pitched upon, but its curious history and strange changes of meaning are of much interest to ourselves, and cannot, as we believe, fail to stimulate the imagination of such of our readers as do not happen to be already in possession of the facts which we are about to lay before them.

The word HEARSE or HERSE, for both forms are recognized by those who are authorities on the subject of spelling, has for modern people, who have not devoted themselves to word-studies. but one meaning. When they hear it, the mind-picture produced is that of a funeral car, with its black trappings and nodding plumes, in which the bodies of the dead are borne to burial. If they have visited Northern Germany or the Netherlands, they may perhaps add to this mental sketch the white skulls and cross-bones painted on the panels, and a driver clad in a long black cloak, with a quilted frill round his neck, such as we see represented in pictures of men who were old, or at least middle-aged, when James the First was king.

HEARSE may, like by far the greater number of words we use, be traced back to an Aryan root. We shall not, however, go further backwards up the stream of time, on the present occasion, than to the days of the Romans.

The most remote ancestor we shall claim for our word on the present occasion is *Hirpex*, the Latin term for a harrow or rake. This word *Hirpex*, though not identical, was, it is evident, near of kin to *Ericius* or *Hericius*, a hedgehog, a term which got to be employed metaphorically by writers on the art of war to indicate a military engine of the nature of a portcullis. In the Commentaries of Cæsar we have " erat objectus portis ericius," * and Sallust says " eminebant in modum ericii militaris veruta binum pedum." †

We have no clear notion of what was the exact form of the Roman *Hirpex*, but until quite recent days, when a great change has taken place, there is nothing in which mankind has been more conservative than in the shapes of agricultural implements. We shall therefore probably not stray far from the truth if we take it for granted that the

* De Bell. Civ. iii. 67.   † Fragm. Lib. iii.

harrows, of which there are a few representations in mediæval illuminations, represent not inaccurately the *Hirpex* of the ancients.

The science of blazonry, too, comes to our aid. An old English family of the surname of Harrow had for its arms three harrows joined together by what the heralds called a wreath, but what is in fact the ring, chain, or rope, by which it was the custom to join them together in triplets. An engraving of this shield is given in John Guillim's *Display* of Heraldry.* They are represented as triangular objects, having three bars running across, into which the tynes or teeth are fixed.

The word HEARSE was occasionally used to indicate the farmer's harrow. Lord Berners, in his admirable translation of Froissart's *Chronicles*, published in 1523, says of a certain battle that "The archers . . . stode in manner of a herse, and the men of armes at the bottom of the bataile." † The first ecclesiastical use of the word is probably due to France, but, if so, it was soon imported into this country. It signifies a triangular frame of wood, which was suspended by a cord or chain from the roof of the Church. In form it would seem to have been just like a harrow, but

* 5th edit., 1679, p. 214.   † Vol I., ch. cxxx., p. 156.

at the points where the bars crossed each other there were sockets in which to put candles. These hearses soon gave way, except, perhaps, in poor churches, to chandeliers of metal, but the hearse only changed its place. It was taken down from above-head, mounted on a stand or post, and used in the service of *Tenebrae*. Then it usually held twenty-four lights, but the custom was by no means everywhere the same. Sometimes this hearse was constructed to carry fourteen yellow candles, with one of white wax in the centre. The yellow candles symbolized the eleven faithful apostles and the three Marys, the white candle in the middle representing our Blessed Lord. In the *Tenebrae* services of mediæval England fourteen psalms were said. As each one was ended a candle was put out. When the time arrived that the white taper alone remained burning, it was concealed behind or near the altar, so as to leave the church in darkness.

When the people had got accustomed to connect the word hearse with a frame for holding candles, it required but a short step to arrive at a new meaning. Prayers for the dead were the universal custom throughout the mediæval Church. When a corpse was brought to church for burial it was placed near to, or at least in sight of, the altar. Over the body, which was usually without a coffin, except in the case of persons of high position, a light frame-work of wood was placed, on which the pall was spread. These frames were a regular part of the church's furniture ; at the corners, and sometimes on the ridge also, there were sockets for candles. To these frames the word hearse was soon applied. They occur frequently in ecclesiastical inventories. In the early part of the reign of Elizabeth we find mention of them in several Lincolnshire churches, e.g., Alkborough, Newton, and Ripingale.* Of these hearses, not a single example is known to have come down to our time. Their fragile nature would render them peculiarly liable to destruction, and they had become mere lumber when prayers for the dead were no longer used by the Established Church. Occasionally, however, these wooden hearses were copied in metal, and made permanent parts of the tombs of persons whose last resting-place was in the Church. A few examples of hearses of this kind have survived the storms of upwards of three hundred years. A very graceful hearse of this

* Peacock, Engl. Church Furniture, pp. 36, 118, 127.

sort still canopies the tomb of one of the Marmions in the Church of Tanfield, near Ripon. It has attached to it sconces for holding seven candles, two on each side, and three on the ridge. A portion of another of singularly beautiful design, which was long ago cast out of the church of Snarford in Lincolnshire, is now in the South Kensington Museum. The effigy of Richard, Earl of Warwick, who died in 1439, possesses a hearse of this kind. It is smaller than those we have already mentioned, but is made of brass, or rather of that mixed metal our forefathers called latten. The contract for making it still exists, and it is noteworthy that it is therein spoken of as a hearse,* shewing that before the middle of the fifteenth century, hearse had become the re-cognised term.

The next step in the progress of word-growth was to apply the term hearse to a temporary canopy of timber, decorated with a profusion of tapers, and draped with hangings and banners bearing heraldic and religious ornaments. This was placed over the body while the funeral rites were being performed. It has been known in every· country of Western Europe, but England

* Parker, Gloss. of Architecture, ed. 1850, vol. 1, p. 250.

is, so far as we know, the country wherein it was called a hearse. *Chapelle ardente* is the ordinary French term. We find *Catafalco* in Italian, and *Castrum doloris* in the Latin of the Church. When the bodies had to be carried a long distance, it was the custom in the case of rich families to erect one of these hearses in every church where it rested for the night. Minute accounts of several of these have come down to us, showing that they were sumptuously decorated. They were, however, we may be sure, never in common use. Chaucer knew these hearses well ; as he spent much of his life in court society he must have seen several of them. In his *Dream* he has given a description of the prayers which were offered up around them :—

> " And after that about the herses,
> Many orisons and verses,
> Without note full softly
> Said, were, and that full heartily,
> That all the night, till it was day,
> The people in the church can pray,
> Unto the Holy Trinity,
> On those soules to have pity."

Though public prayers for the dead were abolished when the new ritual came into force, yet the use of these sumptuous hearses was long retained. They seem to have been employed as a mark of social dignity, and as a means of heraldic display. In 1589, a violent Puritan satire against the then existing order of things in Church and State was issued from a secret press, bearing the strange title of *Pappe with a Hatchet*, wherein the following passage occurs :—

> " Now you put me in minde of the matter, there is a booke coming out of a hundred merrie tales, and the petigree of Matin, fetchte from the burning of Sodome ; his armes shall be set on his hearse, for we are providing for his funeral." *

In William Habingdon's *Castara*, we find the lines :—

> " Lily, Rose, and Violet,
>   Shall the perfumed hearse beset,"

which shows that flowers were sometimes used as a means of decoration. Love knots, too, had a place there. Dryden makes one of his characters say :—

> " And maidens when I die
> Upon my hearse white true-love-knots should lie ;
> And thus my tomb should be inscribed above,
> Here the forsaken virgin rests from love." *

That these stationary hearses were well known to everyone in the middle of the seventeenth

* Ed., 1844, p. 17.   * Marriage-a-la-mode, Act II., Sc. 1

century is proved by the title of the sermon preached by Richard Vines on the death of the Earl of Essex, the Parliamentary general at the beginning of the great Civil War. It runs thus :—

> " The Hearse of the Renowned and Right Honourable Robert, Earl of Essex, and sometime Captain-General of the Armies raised for the Defence of Kinge and Parliament, as represented in his Funerall Sermon, preached at Westminster, 1646."

That stationary hearses were in use at the funerals of the upper classes, so late as 1681, is made evident by a passage in a sermon preached by Nathaniel Resburg, in that year, at the burial of Sir Alan Broderick. The preacher told his hearers that the dead knight had made provision in his will, " that his herse should by no means be garnish'd with the usual ornaments of a family, and no escutcheon should either there or elsewhere appear.*

The funeral car or chariot, to which we now give the name of hearse, to the exclusion of the older meanings, originally differed but very little from these stationary hearses, except that it was upon wheels, and the necessities of locomotion

*. Page 18.

required it to be smaller. We are not aware that there is any evidence that these wheeled hearses were in use in earlier days. There is no reason why they should not have been, but it is probable that the bodies of all but the very great, if they had far to travel, would be conveyed in an ordinary waggon. *

The body of Colonel Rainborowe, the Parliamentarian officer, who was so basely murdered at Doncaster, on the 29th of October, 1648, by desperadoes from the Royalist Garrison, in Pontefract Castle, † seems to have been conveyed from the place where he fell to Wapping, then a village in the outskirts of London, in a hearse.

Milton, in his " Epitaph on the Marchioness of Winchester," when he introduces the word, implies a movable structure.

> " Gentle lady, may thy grave
> Peace and quiet ever have ;
> After this thy travel sore,
> Sweet rest seize thee evermore.

* In Lincolnshire, and we imagine elsewhere, it is frequent for waggons to be used for funereal purposes, by those families which are practically connected with the cultivation of the land, and so possess them of their own.

† A Memoir of this brave soldier, and upright gentleman, containing many of his letters, has been compiled by the present writer, and appears in the *Archæologia*, vol. xlvi.

> " Here be tears of perfect moan
>   Wept for thee in Helicon,
>   And some flowers and some bays
>   For thy herse to strew the ways."

Anthony Walker, a clergyman of the Established Church, preaching in 1673, said that " more friends attend an hearse to the towne-end than will drive through with it the whole journey ; "* and in 1690, they had become one of the necessities of civilization, for we find in that year an advertisement in *The London Gazette*, offering them for hire.

We have accomplished our task by furnishing our readers with a sketch of the evolution of the word Hearse through many centuries, until its meaning has become settled as we now know it. We must not conclude, however, without directing attention to what we consider no legitimate development, but a disease of language. We mean the habit, not uncommon in the seventeenth century, of using hearse in the sense of a dead body. Thomas Heywood, in his *Brytaines Troy*, 1609, says :

> " Now grew the battell hot, bold Archas pierces,
>   Thrugh the mid-hoast and strewes the way with Herses."†

Many similar examples of this perversion, as we

---

* Lees Lacrymans, p. 10.   † Canto 3, st. 86, fol. 72,

regard it, might be produced, but no good end would be served by quoting them.

A dialectic use of the word hearse must not pass unnoticed. A writer in *The Gentleman's Magazine* for the year 1861, says that herse signifies a "crib of wattles," used to protect the banks of the Severn against the encroachments of the tide. * We have never seen one of these objects, but conjecture that they are, or have been, originally made in the form of a harrows.

* Gent. Mag. Lib. Eng., Topog. pt. iv., p. 217.

Heart Burials of English Persons.

BY EMILY SOPHIA HARTSHORNE.

ANTIQUARIES regret, as time proceeds, the loss of many of those varied relics which gladden their heart, and but for tradition, ancient chronicles, and county histories, we should be left very much in ignorance of the days of old.

So those who love the past, and follow step by step the progress of civilization and new customs, must rejoice that some memories are retained of those who are gone, and whose deeds live to record their actions and their honoured names. Our subject, however, only refers to a special object : that of heart burial in England, or with reference to English people, who have signified their wish that this portion of their mortal frame should receive sepulture apart from the body As this was easy to transport, it was considered a safe and certain means of having the heart—maybe one which had known many cares and sorrows —transmitted to the place where affection dictated, and where it would be regarded with reverence and love, and where human tears could be shed over the casket or urn, or in whatever form the heart was encased.

HEART AND FORGET-ME-NOTS,
LINCOLN CATHEDRAL.

By the Crusaders this custom appears to have been instituted, as we learn that from the Holy Land the earliest instances are recorded, both by these precious relics being taken back to the native country, or of being deposited in Palestine's sanctified soil,

"The brave who sleep in soil of thine,
Die not entomb'd, but shrined, O Palestine."

Amongst the earliest instances of heart burials, (we refer to the twelfth century), we read of Stephen, Earl of Brittany and Richmond, who commanded the rear of the conqueror's army at Hastings. He was a man of peace, a lover of the poor, and an honourer of religion. He died in 1104, and directed that his heart should be placed in the Abbey of St. Martin's at York, to which he had been a great benefactor. In 1118, Robert de Mellent, Earl of Leicester, desired that his heart should be placed in a stone depository at Brackley, in Northamptonshire (where he had founded a hospital), and kept in salt. The

15

Bishop of Winchester, who died in 1129, directed that his heart should be placed in a stone depository, in two leaden dishes, where it was found at Waverley Abbey, undecayed and preserved with spices. In the same year Edith, wife of Robert D'Oiley, who had previously founded a Priory of Canons Augustines at Oxford, caused her heart to be there interred, and she is represented upon her tomb holding it in her hand.

William, third Earl of Warren, who fought against the Turks in the second crusade in the Holy Land, where he was slain, caused his heart to be transmitted to England, and deposited in Lewis Priory.

William Mandeville, Earl of Essex, who died at Gisors, 1190, desired that his body should be conveyed to England. Being told that the difficulty of the passage was such that it could not be done, he replied, " If you cannot, it is because you have no mind to do what I, a dying man, desire; then take my heart and carry it thither." Accordingly, it was buried in the Chapter House at Walden in Essex.

William de Longo-Campa, Bishop of Ely, caused his heart to be brought from Poictiers, where he died, and deposited in his cathedral.

This brings us to the end of the twelfth century, and amongst the earliest records in the following one, we find that King John, who died in 1216, had directed that his heart should be buried at the Cistercian Abbey of Crokesden in Staffordshire. The heart of another Earl of Essex (1228) was sent by his Countess to the Chapter House at Walden. Margaret, wife of the Earl of Winchester, who had great affection for Brackley, directed that her heart should be there enshrined within St. John's Hospital. The heart of William, third Earl of Albini, who built Belvoir Castle, had sep- ulture there, and that of

BRASS, ELMSTEAD CHURCH, ESSEX.

his son William, the fourth Earl, subsequently at the same place. Richard Poore, Bishop of Durham, one of King John's executors, was buried with this inscription : " Ibique cor ejus corpus vero apud Durham humatum est," which was extant in Leland's time.

The heart of Bishop des Roches, of Winchester, who was also one of King John's
executors, was sent to Waverley Abbey. That
of Isabel, Countess of Gloucester, in 1239, was
placed in a silver gilt cup at Tewkesbury.

Ethelmarus, Bishop of Winchester, who died
in 1261, is represented in his cathedral with his
crosier, and holding a heart in his hands.

Senechia, Countess of Cornwall, departed this
life in 1262. Her heart received sepulture at
Cirencester. Robert de Gourney's heart was
interred in the church of Friars Preachers at
Bristol in 1269. Henry, son of Richard, King of
the Romans and Earl of Cornwall, went to the
Holy Land. On his way home, in 1270, he was
slain in Tuscany when attending mass in the
church of St. Lawrence. His father caused his
heart to be honourably placed in a gilt cup, near
the coffin of St. Edward, in Westminster Abbey.
Sir Roger de Leyburn was one of the most stirring
and distinguished warriors of the day, whose
whole life was passed between the tilting lists and
the battlefield.

Sir Roger, the servant of Henry III., and the
trusty friend of Prince Edward, went to the Holy
Land. Wherever he may have died, we know

CROKESDEN ABBEY.

for certain that his death had occurred before the end of November, A.D. 1271, and it is more than probable that Prince Edward took care that his heart was enshrined at Leybourne, as on examination of the heart shrine in that church, there is every reason to believe that his heart was laid to rest there.

Again, in 1272, Richard, King of the Romans, Earl of Cornwall, who had undertaken a second journey to the Holy Land, died. His fourth wife, Beatrix Falkeston, deposited his heart, under a sumptuous pyramid of wonderful workmanship, in the Church of Friars Minors, at Oxford, which had been beautified and enlarged at the expense of herself and her husband. The same year we read that Ralph de Scopham's, Lord of Bryanston, heart was buried under the font in his church, in Dorsetshire, with this brief inscription :—

"Hic jacet cor Radulphi de Scopham."

In 1274, the heart of Robert de Sutton, a Monk of Peterborough, was brought in a cup to his Monastery, and there buried before the altar of St. Oswald.

The Bishop of Winchester, Nicholas de Ely, directed that his heart should be entombed in the south wall of the Presbytery of Winchester, where it was placed in 1280, with the following inscription :—

"Intus est cor Nicholai olim episcopi cujus corpus est apud Waverlie."

The heart of Thomas Cantelupe was enshrined with great honour in the Chapel of Our Lady in his cathedral at Hereford, 1282.

The death of Alphonso, son of Edward I. and Queen Eleanor, was a great affliction to his royal parents, and they caused his heart to receive sepulture in the Church of the Black Friars', London, 1284.

Robert de Ros, Lord of Belvoir, who raised a new battlement to the Castle of Belvoir, deceased in June, 1285. His heart had sepulture at Belvoir.

The heart of Hugh de Batsham, Bishop of Ely in 1286, was placed near the altar of St. Martin, at Ely.

The heart of Eleanor of Provence, wife of Henry III., was interred with great solemnity in London, in the church belonging to the Minor Brothers, 1290.

Eleanor of Castille, the heroic wife of Edward I., and the most devoted of consorts, was buried at the feet of Henry III., in Westminster Abbey, in December, 1290, and, two days after, her heart was deposited in the Church of Black Friars, London.

William Beauchamp, Earl of Warwick, who died 1298, requested that his heart should be taken wheresoever the Countess, his dear consort, should herself resolve to be interred.   The hearts of John and Margaret, children of William Valence, were taken to the Black Friars' Church, in London, the interment of which is mentioned with that of Alphonso, son of Edward I., who was related to them.

We now pass on to 1300, and find at an early date that the heart of Maude de Hastings was buried before the High Altar, at Barnwell Priory, Cambridgeshire.

Edward I., whose heart had known such intense sorrow for the death of his beloved Eleanor, expressed a much more pious wish with respect to his heart than he did with regard to the disposal of his body, as he desired this might be sent to the Holy Land, since he would not go in person according to his vow, and that it should be deposited at Jerusalem, with thirty-two thousand pounds sterling, which he had provided for the support of the Holy Sepulchre, to be taken thence with a noble retinue.

Stow, in his Survey of London, states that in the midst of the Church of the Grey Friars, London, is an alabaster tomb, containing the body of Queen Isabella, with the heart of her husband on her breast; also that of Peter Mountford in the same church, says the same author.

Early in the fifteenth century, the heart of Sir Hugh Mortimer received sepulture in Reading Abbey. In the Church of Burford, Shropshire, a simple tomb records that the heart of Edmond Cornwall, Esquire, lies within it—

> "O Lord, my contrite heart and meek,
> Do not refuse, I Thee beseek."

William, Lord Botreau, a great benefactor of religious houses, directed his heart to be buried at Bridgewater, 1462, and that of Anthony Woodville, Earl Rivers, was by desire carried to our Lady of Pue, at Westminster.

With the sixteenth century, we learn that the heart of the young Prince Arthur of Wales, was buried in the Church of Ludlow. Some years ago the silver box in which it was encased was taken up, and the heart was found to be double. The case was embezzled by the sexton.

Eleanor, Duchess of Buckingham, appointed that her heart should be buried before the image of St. Francis, in the Church of the Grey Friars, London. She died in 1531.

The heart of Queen Mary, the daughter of Henry VIII., was interred in Westminster Abbey, where subsequently that of Queen Elizabeth was taken, in 1670. When the royal vault was opened, the urns containing them were found within the niches, having their names inscribed upon them.

The heart of Sir Robert Peckham, who died at Rome, 1569, was discovered at Denham, Buckinghamshire, in 1711, in a small box of lead fashioned like a heart, flat and soldered, and wrapped with several cloths still smelling strong of the embalment. On the lid was written this inscription :—

> "I.H.S. Robertus Peckham Egnes Auratus Anglus cor summ Dulciss, patrie major. Monumentis commendari Obitt idie September MDLXIX."

In 1575 died Edward, Earl of Windsor, abroad, but his heart was enclosed in lead, and sent to England to be buried under his father's tomb, in token of a true Englishman.

Captain Thomas Hodges, on receiving his last wound in 1583, gave three legacies ; his soul to his Lord Jesus, his body to be lodged in Flemish earth, his heart to be sent to his dear wife in England. At Wedmore, Somerset, is a monument to his memory, bearing the following inscription :—

" Here lies his wounded heart
For whom
One kingdom was too small
A room ;
Two kingdoms therefore have
Thought fit to part
So stout a body and so brave a heart."

In 1586 died Sir Henry Sidney, Earl of Leicester. The leaden urn or cup containing his heart was carried to Ludlow and deposited in the same tomb with his dearly loved daughter Ambrosia, in the little oratory he had made in the church

URN CONTAINING THE HEART OF SIR HENRY SIDNEY.

of St. Lawrence. The seventeenth century records, in 1600, the heart of Anna Sophia Harley, the infant daughter of the French Ambassador, which was deposited in a gilt cup or vase, and placed upon a pyramid of marble in St. Nicholas' Chapel, Westminster Abbey.

The heart burial of Henry, Prince of Wales, who died at eighteen, took place in 1612. His heart was enclosed in lead, and placed upon his breast in Westminster Abbey.

CARVING ON A FINIAL IN BRINGTON CHURCH.

At the church of Brington, Northamptonshire, the parish in which Atthorp is situated, is a leaden drum deposited in the wall, which is supposed to contain the heart of Henry, Lord Spencer, Earl of Sunderland, who died in 1643.

The heart of Arthur, Lord Chapel, who, in 1648, submitted to his death upon the scaffold with unparalleled Christian courage, was deposited in a silver box enclosed in another with two locks, which was subsequently placed in an iron box and deposited in the family vault. In 1656, the heart of Admiral Blake, who had died in the harbour, was embalmed, and buried in St. Andrew's Church at

Plymouth. That of Isabella, Countess of Northampton, was placed in the Sackville vault, in the
church of Withyam, Sussex, in a leaden case in
the shape of a heart, on a brass plate affixed to
which is inscribed :—

> "The Hart of Isabella, Countess of
> Northampton.
> Died the 14th of October, 1661."

In the same year the heart of Esme Stuart, Duke
of Richmond, was enshrined in St. Nicholas'
Chapel, Westminster Abbey.

Sir Nicholas Crispe, a wealthy citizen of
London, who built the church of Hammersmith
in the time of King Charles I., had placed under
an effigy of the King on a pedestal an urn with
this inscription :—

> "Within this urn is entombed the heart of Sir Nicholas
> Crispe, Knight and Baronet, a loyal sharer in the suffer-
> ings of his late and present Majesty. He first settled the
> trade of gold from Guinea, and then built the Castle of
> Cormantin. Died the 28th of July, 1665, aged 67."

In 1685, Arthur Capel's (Earl of Essex, son of
the heroic Lord Capel) heart was enclosed in a
marble heart case, and kept at the family seat,
Cashiobury. The heart of Charles the Second
received sepulture in Westminster Abbey enclosed

in a silver case covered with purple velvet, and placed upon his coffin. The heart of Mary II., Queen of England, was also treated in a similar way, and placed upon her coffin in the vault of Henry the Seventh's Chapel in Westminster Abbey. Sir William Temple, who died in 1699, selected for his heart's resting-place a sunny spot under the sundial, opposite to the window of an apartment from which he used to contemplate the works of Nature, and there it was placed in a silver box. In the year 1702 we record that the heart of William III., King of England, was enclosed in silver, covered with purple velvet, and placed upon his coffin in Westminster Abbey, and that of Prince George of Denmark

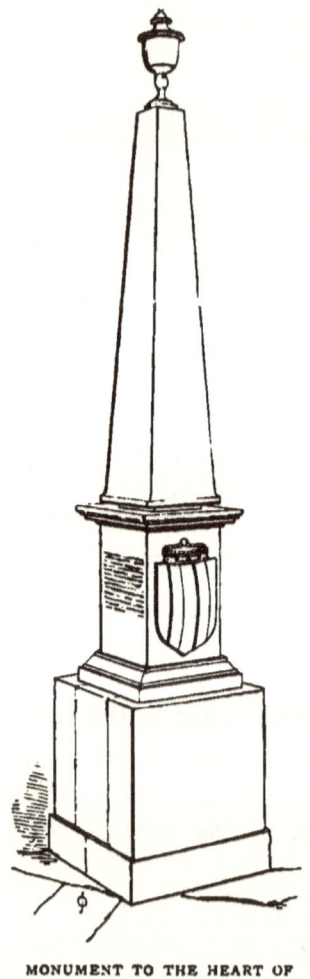

MONUMENT TO THE HEART OF
ANNA SOPHIA HARLEY.

in a like manner at the same place. Queen Anne's heart received sepulture in 1714, also encased in silver, and covered with purple velvet.

In the Columbarium, under the mausoleum at Maulden Church, Bedfordshire, are two urns containing "the hearts of Thomas, Earl of Ailsbury, and his second Lady," date 1741.

In 1755, we know that the heart of the well-known antiquary, Dr. Richard Rawlinson, was bequeathed by him to St. John's College, Oxford, where it is placed in a beautiful marble urn.

To Paul Whitehead, Esquire, of Twickenham, we find the following obiit, December 30, 1774 :

> "Unhallowed hands this urn forbear,
> No gems nor orient spoil
> Lie here conceal'd, but what more rare—
> A heart that knew no guile."

The year 1822 points out to us that the poet Percy Bysshe Shelley, whose body was washed on shore in the Gulf of Spizia, was, according to Italian custom, burnt. The heart, however, would not consume, and was placed in an urn and deposited in the English Protestant burial ground at Rome :—

> "Born August 5, 1792,
> Died July 8, 1822."
> "Cor Cordium."

The same remarkable circumstance took place when Archbishop Cranmer was brought to the stake. His heart was not once touched by the fire, and was found amongst his ashes after his body was consumed.

The heart of George Gordon, Lord Byron, who died at Missolonghi, in 1824, was sent to England for interment, enclosed in a silver urn. It was not placed in the family vault at Newstead as was supposed, but in the chancel of Hucknall Torkard Church, with an inscription upon the box in which it was enclosed.

This must close our list of English heart burials, although there are many more ; yet it is sufficient to state these tell us much that is sad, much that is interesting, and where, in those singular and strange receptacles, the ingenuity of man has fondly sought to preserve these remnants of mortality from the power of oblivion and decay. We desire to echo a piteous response for those now calmly sleeping, and by their works of piety revive and hallow their memory.

> " Theirs are enshrined names, and every heart
> Shall bear the blazon'd impress of their worth."

Boy=Bishops.

By England Howlett.

O F the many bygone festivals which at one time were so popular in England, and which from one cause or another have gradually fallen into such oblivion as to be almost forgotten, perhaps few, if any, held for so long a period such a fascination for all classes of people throughout the length and breadth of the country as the ceremonial incident to the election, and mimic pontificate, of the boy-bishops. No doubt the fact that all the participators in the observance of this curious custom were children would strongly appeal to the feelings of the people, who would, not unnaturally, crowd together to see with what solemnity and dignity these children could imitate the office of the highest ecclesiastical dignitaries. It would certainly seem that in the olden days some good must have resulted from the observance of the ceremonial, for it received support from nearly every church throughout the land, and also support from the monasteries.

16

In the Middle Ages, when festivities and pageantry were so popular as almost to form a necessary part of existence, St. Nicholas' Day (6th December) took a very prominent place; this day being set apart for the election of boy-bishops in various parts of the country. This practice was not confined to cathedral cities alone, but boy-bishops were elected from colleges, grammar schools, and parish churches. As patron of scholars, St. Nicholas had a double feast at Eton College, where the scholars, to avoid in anyway interfering with the boy-bishop on St. Nicholas' Day, elected their boy-bishop in November on St. Hugh's Day.

This festival in various forms seems to have been celebrated in most, if not all, Christian countries, therefore it naturally assumed very different complexions according to time and place; in some instances the ceremony was of a purely serious and religious character, and in others it verged closely on the burlesque and profane. In all places this childish pageantry appears to have appealed strongly to the people, and so great were the crowds which assembled to witness the processions and mimic pontifical ministrations, that it was specially provided by the statute of Sarum that no one was to press upon the children or interrupt them during their procession or service in the cathedral upon pain of anathema.

In the early days of this festival in honour of St. Nicholas, there is no doubt but that it was intended solely as a reverential observance, but it was impossible that such a farce could for any length of time be taken seriously either by the children taking part in it, or the people who thronged to witness it. That the show maintained its popularity to the last is amply proved, but the wonder is that the Church did not sooner awake to the fact that this playing at bishops was certainly not in anyway conducive to the dignity of those who properly held the office.

The boy-bishop was elected annually on St. Nicholas' Day; he was generally a chorister, and elected by members of the choir. His term of office sometimes only lasted until Holy Innocents' Day, but in other cases for a much longer period, the title itself being held until the next election. According to the custom of Salisbury, the *Episcopus Puerorum* was chosen by his fellow children, and he held all the state of a true bishop. After the election, the boy-bishop was vested in full episcopal vestments, with mitre, ring, and pastoral staff. In some cases he entered the church or cathedral, and performed episcopal functions there, even going through a form not unlike what has been called "Table Prayers" in the Church of England; that is, celebration of mass without any consecration.

At Salisbury, in the procession of the boy-bishop, the dean and residentiaries went first, followed by the chaplains, the bishop, and petty prebendaries. The choristers sat in the upper stalls, the residentiaries furnished the incense and book, and the petties were taper-bearers. The boy-bishop exacted ceremonial obedience from his fellows, who, dressed like priests, performed all the ceremonies and offices which might have been celebrated by a bishop and his prebendaries.

In the diocese of York, as early as 1367, it was ordered as an indispensable requisite, " that the bishop of the boys should, for the future, be he who had served longest in the church, and who should be most suitable, provided, nevertheless, that he was sufficiently handsome in person, and that any election otherwise should not be valid." It would seem, therefore, that good looks were indispensable requisites for every candidate for the youthful bishopric.

The boy-bishops made visitations to various places in their diocese. These appear to have been lucrative, as well, no doubt, as pleasant excursions, especially at the hands of the local nobility, whose welcome guests they were. On December 7th, 1229, a boy-bishop, in the chapel at Heton, near Newcastle-on-Tyne, said vesper before Edward I. on his way to Scotland, who made considerable presents to him and the other boys who sang with him. In 1319, Roger de Mortival, Bishop of Salisbury, found it necessary to curtail some of the observances. He forbade both feast and visitation, and, in some places, the boys were kept from wandering beyond parish bounds.

In 1396, John de Cave, boy-bishop of York, went on his visitation tour. He was attended by a considerable retinue, and his accounts were kept by Nicholas, of Newark, "Guardian of the property of the boy-bishop." It seems to have been a succession of excursions from and back to York. When the accounts were balanced, and the receipt of gifts weighed against expenses, there remained forty

shillings and sixpence halfpenny for the little bishop
to put in his pocket, a considerable sum in those
days, considering the relative value of money.

It does not seem quite clear at what period this
idle ceremony was first established, but probably
it was ancient, and at least it can be traced back
with certainty to the thirteenth century.

With respect to vestments, etc., used by the
boy-bishop and his companions, there are many
notices of these in cathedral and parish records.
In the will of Thomas Rotheram, Archbishop of
York, dated in 1481, is a bequest to the college of
that place of a mitre of cloth of gold, with two
silver enamelled " knoppes," to be worn by the
"*Barnes Bishop*." In a MS. inventory of vestments, committed to the care of the Sacristan of
Magdalen College, Oxford, in 1495, are "*pro
peuris*" tunicles, red and white and crimson, with
orfreys of damask and velvet, one set of albs of
blue damask, and two with apparels of red silk,
and, lastly, a banner of St. Nicholas. The
churchwardens' accounts of St. Mary-at-Hill,
London, 10 Henry VI., make mention of "two
children's copes, also a myter of cloth of gold set
with stones."

It would seem as though the Boy Bishops

either each had a new seat or throne, or that the one provided required constant repair. The following extracts are taken from the Louth Churchwardens' accounts :—

> 1500. Paid to the Chyld Byshop at Cristynmes for j paire cloffes, 1d.
> To Thomas Couper, ijd. John Bradpull, ijd., and making his See ov. nayles.
> 1501. Paid for one Chyld Bishop j pair cloffes. Making his See, vjd.
> 1505. Paid for making the Child Bishop See, vjd.

On the Feast of Holy Innocents, the Boy Bishop delivered a sermon, which, although couched in somewhat childish language, was doubtless prepared by some dignitary of the church. This ancient custom was not only allowed and continued by the founders of Winchester and Eton, but when Dean Colet made the laws for his Grammar School, in the year 1512, he directed that his scholars should on every Childermas day hear the child bishop's sermon in Paul's, and afterwards, attending the High Mass, offer each of them one penny to the child-bishop. This was done no doubt as a stimulus to Christian ambition in the boys, just as the mitre and staff are painted, as the rewards of learning, on the school walls of Winchester.

It appears to have been usual that money should be struck for the boy-bishop—"St. Nicholas pence"—it was called. In the church of St. Mary, at Bury St. Edmund's, there was a Guild of St. Nicholas; and in the year 1842, during the removal of the priest's stalls, a quantity of leaden pieces, formed in imitation of money, were discovered; these were undoubtedly relics commemorative of the boy-bishop.

In case a boy-bishop died within a month of his election, his obsequies were solemnized with glorious pomp and sadness. He was buried, like all other bishops, in his vestments and ornaments. In Salisbury Cathedral, there is a diminutive effigy of a bishop in full canonicals, and this is popularly believed to be the tomb of a boy-bishop; the figure is about three feet in length, and the name of the person represented is not known. It seems, however, probable that it is the monument of one of the earlier bishops, who are known to have been buried in the Cathedral, but the place of whose interment is not known. The Salisbury Chapter memorials contain many references to the boy-bishops, in which the name of the boy is given, and not unfrequently the amount of the money offerings received, but there is not any record of the death of any boy-bishop.

In the year 1541, Henry VIII., by proclamation, abolished the practice of electing boy-bishops, much to the regret of the people, who were thus deprived of what, for so long a period, had been their most popular show, and one which, no doubt, they had come to look upon as being an annual ceremonial to continue for all time ; however, it was hardly to be expected that the puritan spirit of that age could countenance or even permit such a burlesque. Up to this time, what Archbishop Peckham had denounced, at Godstowe, in 1279, the dressing up of girls to publicly read prayers on Innocents' Day, still continued ; but Henry suppressed this also, with other " chyldysh observaunces."

After the accession of Mary, and the re-establishment of the Roman Catholic religion, an order was issued for the going about of the procession of St. Nicholas. For some reason or other, which does not appear, the order was recalled ; but in 1556, the festival, processions, and all the rites and ceremonies of the boy-bishop were fully restored. The youthful prelate, with his retinue and all their paraphernalia, was introduced to the

Queen, and in whose honour he sang a song in her presence. All collegiate churches, and a large number of schools, revived the practice; but the final abolition was near at hand. The half sacred element, which was once connected with the principal actor, died out in the eyes of authorities, who began to see much abuse in this sacro-comic performance.

All came to an end with the death of Mary, and no longer the boys of Paul's obeyed the order of their founder, Dean Colet, to attend at Childermas and listen to the boy-bishop's sermon. The popular festival died hard, but a period of three hundred years has not effaced the interest incident to the ceremony, although it is now well-nigh shrouded by the mists of antiquity.

Gleanings from a Parish Chest.

By Rev. J. Charles Cox, LL.D., F.S.A.

PARISH chests, which were almost invariably kept in the parish church, as the safest possible place for their preservation, were used as the store-holds for most interesting and valuable classes of documents, for centuries before the days of the Reformation. In such places, were not only kept the charters and evidences that pertained to lands given for the purpose of maintaining lights in the church, and for other like ecclesiastical purposes, but also, in many cases, documents of still greater value to the parish at large, such as the manor court rolls, that regulated all the affairs of village and community life.

In searching among a great number of our village parish chests, stores of such rolls are even now occasionally found ; we have met with them from early fourteenth century days, in the chests of Alrewas and Yoxall, Staffordshire.

After the parochial legislation of the close of

Elizabeth's reign, parish books and accounts began to multiply, and the well-kept parish chest will be found to contain the separate accounts of churchwardens, overseers of the poor, parish constables, and way-wardens.

From time to time search will be rewarded by a strange variety of unexpected scraps and fragments, that may throw some little light not only on local customs, but even on national history. During the last thirty years, we have opened the lids and searched with more or less diligence into hundreds of village and town chests, and though not infrequently some wretched spirit of modern neatness or utilitarianism has cleared out every document and book, and left perchance nothing more savoury than smelling paraffin cans and noisome lamp wick, still as a rule the search is well repaid (particularly when we are assured there is nothing of value), and occasionally delightful finds are the reward of patient persistence and considerable trouble.

But never do we expect to find so rich a variety of unexpected treasures and scraps as rewarded our efforts in April, 1864, when we handled the first contents of the first parish chest that came under our notice. In clearing

out a large, roughly-made, lidless chest, beneath
the tower of the parish church of Luccombe,
Somerset, wherein the sexton kept his tools, a
considerable store of decaying papers came to
light, beneath a mildewed parish pall.   The first
thing that attracted attention was a small roll in
which were tightly wrapped in the blank parch-
ment leaf of a register book, and fastened round
with a leathern thong, a 1643 Form of Prayer
and Thanksgiving issued by the king at Oxford,
together with special thanksgivings for the birth
of Charles II., in 1630, and of the Princess
Mary in 1631.   Among the heap of papers were
found a variety of post-Restoration and eighteenth
century forms of prayer, several of which, after
painstaking investigation, appear to be absolutely unique copies.   The preservation of the
earliest of these forms of prayer in this out-of-
the-world, though lovely little west country
village, which nestles in the offshoots of Exmoor,
under the shadow of Dunkery Beacon, is
accounted for when we recollect the parsons
who were once rectors of Luccombe.   In 1575,
Queen Elizabeth presented Laurence Byam, one
of an old Monmouthshire family of note, to this
rectory, which he held for nearly forty years,

dying in 1614. Three of his four sons became distinguished divines. Henry, the eldest, born at Luccombe, in 1580, "one of the greatest ornaments of the University," says Wood, in his *Athenæ*, succeeded his father in the living of Luccombe. He resided at Luccombe, though holding other preferments, and was proctor in convocation for his diocese. At the beginning of the civil war, he took so active a part for the crown, that troops were dispatched to arrest him. Escaping from the Roundheads, Henry Byam joined the king at Oxford, in 1642. Dr. Byam's devotion to the royal cause was strongly echoed by his family. Four of his five sons were captains in the king's armies, two of them losing their lives in battle. His wife and daughter, when trying to escape the persecution of the Roundheads (whilst Dr. Byam was at Oxford), by crossing the Bristol Channel into Wales, were both of them drowned. When Prince Charles, afterwards Charles II., fled from England, Dr. Byam accompanied him to the Scilly Islands, and afterwards to Jersey, as his chaplain. He was also for a time with Charles at the Hague. At the restoration, he was reinstated in the benefice of Luccombe, and made Canon of Exeter and Prebendary of Wells. It was only his modesty that prevented him from being made Bishop. He died in 1669, aged 81, having been rector of Luccombe for 55 years. Father and son had thus held that benefice for only six years short of a century.

We have already given full descriptions of the highly interesting series of Forms of Prayer and Thanksgiving, in the occasional accompanying proclamations, that were discovered in this chest, in four articles, in vols. vii. and viii. of the *Newbery House Magazine*, but nothing has hitherto been made known with regard to other curious contents of this parochial chest. We now proceed to deal with the more noteworthy of these odds and ends.

The earliest fragments of a document found in this chest contained a list of high officials of the kingdom, followed by a list of bishops according to their precedence. How these two leaves came to be deposited in such a place it would be idle now to conjecture. They have evidently formed part of some large manuscript book, carefully written. There is no date on these pages, but from the names mentioned, and from the fact of the sees of Oxford and Bristol being vacant, it is clear that they, belong to the end of Elizabeth's reign, somewhere between 1593 and 1600. The following is a transcript :—

" The names of the High Commissioners.

Tharchbishopp, Bishopp of London, B. of Durham, B. of Winchester, B. of Elye, B. of Hereford, B. of Coventrie and Lichfeld, B. of Sarum, B. of Lincolne, B. of St. Davies, B. of Peterborough, B. of Worchester, B. of Norwiche, B. of Chichester, and the Bishopp of Rochester for the time being, B. of Carlisle, B. Suffragan of Dover, Lo. Maior of London, Lord Wentworthe, Lo. Ryche, Lord Bathurst, Sr Xpoper Wraye, l. chefe Justice of England, Sir Henry Sidney, Sir Frauncis Knollis, Sr Xpofer Hatton, Sr Frauncis Walsingham, Sr Walter Myldmay, Sr Gilbert errard, M^r of the Rolls, Sr Roger Marwood, L. cheife Baron, John Southcotte armiger mort., William Aliffe armiger, Sr George Carew knight.

The names of the Lordes and others of her Ma'ties Privie Counsell.

Sir Thomas Bromley, Knight, Lord Chaunceldor of England; the Lord Bourleigh, l. Treasurer; the Earle of Lincolne, L. Admirall; the Earle of Shreuesberye, high Marshall of England; the lo. Charles Howard Baron of Effingham, Lo. Chamberlayne of her Maties house; the Earle of Warwick, M^r of the Ordinaunce; the Earle of Bedforde, the Earle of Leicester, M^r of the horse; the lo. Hundsdon, lo. Governor of Barwick, capt. of the Gentlemen Pensioners; Sr Frauncis Knollis, knight, Treasurer of the household; Sr James Acroft, knight, comptroller; Sir Henry Sidney, knight of the order, lo. President of Walles.

A note of the Bishoppes and how they are to take place each
below or after other.

Archbishopp of Canterbury.
Archb. of Yorke.
Bishopp of London.
B. of Winchester.
B. of Duresme.
B. of Hereford.
B. of Elye.
B. of St. Davies.
B. of Salisburye.
Bishopp of Bath and Wells.
B. of Coventrie and Lichfeld.
B. of Peterborough.
B. of Chester.
B. of Gloucester.
B. of Bangor.
B. of Carlisle.
B. of Chichester.
B. of Lincolne.
B. of Exeter.
B. of Worcester.
B. of St. Asaph.
B. of Landaff.
B. of Rochester
Bristoll ⎫
Oxford ⎬ Vacante.

The 2 Archbishoppes so placed of dignitye, the 3 Bps. following so placed by an Act of Parlament.

All that follow have there places as they be putt downe neither by there dignitye nor by Act of Parlament, but according to the severall tymes of there severall Consecretions."

17

In a torn and fragmentary condition, below a
heap of comparatively recent apprentice in-
dentures, was a creased and much-folded paper.
A tedious process removed the creases, and when
mounted it became evident that this was the first
of two consecutive large-sized Parliamentary
broadsheets—which are of great rarity—issued
on 17th April, 1646, in the midst of the great
Civil War struggle, but a few days before the
unhappy and deserted Charles left Oxford in
disguise, with two attendants, on his way to
Newark. The sheet measures eighteen inches
by fifteen inches, and is clearly printed in good
type. It is styled "A Declaration of the
Commons of England assembled in Parliament,
of their true Intentions concerning the Ancient
and Fundamental Government of the Kingdom;
the Government of the Church; the present
Peace; Securing the People against all Arbitrary
Government, and maintaining a right understand-
ing between the Two Kingdoms of England
and Scotland according to the Covenant and
Treaties." The Commons proceed to recite the
objects they had had in view from the beginning
of the war, observing that "when it hath pleased
God to blesse our Endeavours and the Actions of

Our Forces and Armes, as that the Enemy is in dispair to accomplish his designes by War, and We are brought into good hopes of attaining and enjoying that which with so much expense of Blood and Treasure We have contended for"— the same spirits are still stirring as at the beginning to misrepresent their intentions and aims. They state that they are accused of wishing to recede from the solemn league and covenant entered into between the two kingdoms, and of desiring to continue "these uncomfortable troubles and bleeding distractions," in order to leave all government in Church and State loose and unsettled, and to assume for themselves the same arbitrary power over the persons and estates of the subjects, "which this Parliament hath thought fit to abolish by taking away the Star Chamber, High Commissioners, and other Actuary Courts, and the Exorbitant Power of the Council Table."

The Commons, therefore, think well solemnly to repeat what are their true and real intentions. First, with regard to Church government, they note how they had "fully declared for a Presbyterial Government," and passed most of the particulars brought to them from the Assembly of Divines, and had only refrained

from granting arbitrary and unlimited power, and
that it was their resolve still further "to
endeavour the Reformation of Religion in the
kingdoms of England and Ireland, in Doctrine,
Worship, Discipline, and Government, according
to the Word of God, and the Example of the
best Reformed Churches, and according to our
Covenant."

This sheet from the Luccombe chest stops
short in the midst of the declaration about
religion, and it was a long time before we could
discover the conclusion of this valuable historical
utterance. It is not referred to in any of our usual
histories of England, even the fullest, and we
failed to find a copy in several collections of
proclamations. But at last we came across a
folio volume printed by "Ed. Husband, Printer
to the Honorable House of Commons, and sold
at his shop at the signe of the Golden Dragon in
Flete Street nere the Temple Gate, 1646," which
contained a collection of "All the Publick Ordain
Ordinances and Declarations of both Houses of
Parliament from the ninth of March, 1642, untill
December, 1646." From this volume we were
able to recover the remainder of the declaration.
The remainder states that the Commons were in

favour of the continuance of the fundamental constitution and government of the kingdom by King, Lords, and Commons; of depriving the crown of any pretended power of the Militia; by maintaining the abolition of court of wards and liveries, and of all tenures *in capite*, and by knights' service; of reducing garrisons; of bringing delinquents who had fomented the war to due punishment; and of fully observing the solemn league and covenant between the two kingdoms of England and Scotland.

One of the very next orders issued by the parliament, when the news reached them of the flight of the king from Oxford, on April 27th, on an unknown journey, was the following brief statement—by far the shortest that the "long parliament" ever put out—which runs to the following effect :—

"Die Lunæ, 4 Maii, 1646.

Ordered that it be, and it is, hereby Declared by the Lords and Commons in Parliament assembled, that what person soever shall harbor and conceal, or know of the harboring and concealing of the King's person, and shall not reveal it immediately to the Speakers of both Houses, shall be proceeded against as a Traytor to the Commonwealth, forfeit his whole Estate, and dye without Mercy."

On the same day it was ordered that the

committee of the Militia of the city of London be desired to publish the above order by beat of drum or sound of trumpet within the cities of London and Westminster and lines of communication. The order was hardly likely to be sent out save to districts where there was strong reason to suspect that the king might be inclined to make his way or to seek concealment. Why then should this order have found its way to this retired little Somersetshire village of Luccombe? The probable answer is that Luccombe, as has been already remarked, was the residence of that very prominent royalist clergyman, Lawrence Byam, and his family, and that the royalist garrison of Dunster Castle, six miles distant from Luccombe, had but just yielded to the Parliamentarians. An order of the two Houses, dated May 2nd, had just been issued, commanding that May 19th be observed as a day of " Publique Thanksgiving in all places within the power of the Parliament for the several Mercies of God upon the forces of the Parliament in reducing and taking in the several Castles and Garisons of Portland, Ruthyn, Exeter, Barnstaple, the Mount in Cornwall, Dunster Castle, Tutbury and Aberistwith Castles, Woodstock Manor, and the

Castle of Bridgenorth." At Dunster Castle there is still shown a hiding-place, behind the panelling of a bed-chamber, where Charles I. is traditionally said to have been concealed. We believe this brief order of May 4th, found at Luccombe, to be an absolutely unique copy.

In another corner of the chest, crumpled up into a small ball, was a thin printed paper. After careful unrolling and smoothing, it proved to be a somewhat damaged broadsheet, seventeen inches by fifteen inches, printed on one side, with orna- mental heading and initial letter. It was "the humble Petition of Arthur Gwin and Roger Gwin, Ministers of God's word, in behalf of their captivated and distressed families in Ireland," addressed to "the Right Honourable the Lords assembled in Parliament." In the body of the petition it was stated that the petitioners had lost their estates in Ireland "by that horrid and matchless Rebellion " to the value of £2,240, in addition to an annual income of £350, whereby they and their families, numbering sixteen souls were reduced to great want ; that the aged mother and two children of Arthur were captives with the Irish Rebels ; that Roger's wife and five small children were in the city of Cork suffering

extreme want, and without God's special provi-
dence like to perish; and that through their
grievous losses and the sad destruction of the
kindgom they "are utterly disenabled to redeem
and bring away those miserable Captives, and
other distressed persons in whom they are so
nearly concerned." They therefore prayed for
authority "to quietly pass and repass in and about
their specified occasions" for a period of ten
months, and more especially to be recommended to
godly ministers of the gospel that they may
effectually move their congregation to charitable
contributions, "that so they may be in some
possibility to Redeem, relieve, and Fetch away
those poor captivated and distressed Christians
from among the Barbarous Rebels." Appended
to the petition is the certificate of " sundry
Protestant Lords and Noble Personages of the
Kingdom of Ireland," who sign as Kerry,
Ranelagh, Broghill, W. Fenton, and John
Percivall, testifying to the truth of the statements.
At the base of the broadsheet, printed in italics,
is the following parliamentary record :—

" Die Jovis. 3 Septemb., 1646.
Upon the Petition of Arthur Gwin and Roger Gwin,
ministers, read this day in the House, shewing that

(besides their great losses in the Kingdom of Ireland) the said Arthur hath his mother and two children captives with the Irish Rebels, and that Roger Gwin hath his wife and five small Children in the City of Cork ;

It is ordered by the Lords in Parliament assembled, That the Petitioners be permitted to pass into Ireland, and to return back with their said company without the let or hindrance of any person whatsoever.

And that the Ministers of God's Word to whom they shall address themselves, be pleased to move effectually their Congregations charitably to contribute towards the inabling of the said poor petitioners to Relieve, Release, and fetch off the said Captives and other distressed persons, as in their said Petition is expressed.

Joh : Brown, Cleric. Parliamentorum."

Comparatively little is known about post-reformation excommunications in England, although frequently put in force during the seventeenth and eighteenth centuries for technical ecclesiastical offences, and occasionally for moral wrong-doing. So far as we aware, no example of such an excommunication has ever been printed *in extenso*, and therefore no apology is necessary for giving one from the Luccombe chest of the time of Charles I. According to English canon law, a sentence of excommunication was bound to be delivered in writing and under proper seal. This document is written on a half-sheet of foolscap lengthways, and has borne a large vesica-

shaped wafer seal on the left-hand margin, but
nothing now remains of the seal save the stain
where it was originally stamped.

"Samuel Ward doctor of divinity Archdeacon of the
Archdeaconry of Taunton to our well-beloved the Parson
Vicar or Curate of the parish church of Luccombe within
our Archdeaconry of Taunton sendeth greetinge in our
Lord God everlastinge. Whereas Walter Pugslie, Moses
Pugslie, and John Anton of ye parish aforesaid for their
manifest contempte and disobedience have been longe
time justlie excommunicated and for excommunicate
persons openly denounced in the face of the Chuch at the
time of divine service in which dangerous estate without
feare of God or shame of ye world they still remaine in
contempte of lawe and lawful magistrates. We therefore
will and require you that the next Sabath day or holiday
ensuinge the Receipt hereof in your said parish Church at
the time of divine service before the whole congregation
assembled you shall publiquely denounce those Walter
Pugslie Moses Pugslie and John Anton for aggravated
persons and also then and there you shall admonish all
Christian people by virtue hereof that they and any of
them henceforth eschewe and avoid the society, fellow-
shippe and company of the said persons and that they
neither eate, nor drink, buy, sell, or otherwise by any
manner of means communicate with them, being members
cut off from all Christian Society under the payne of
excommunication by lawe in this behalf provided until
they shall submit themselves to be reconciled. And of
y^r doinges herein Certifie us or our Deputy the next court
day ensuinge after fortye dayes after the denouncinge
hereof and fayle you not under the payne contempte.

Dated under our Seale the three and twentye day of May
Anno dom, 1628.

Ric : Peeke Reg."

It is no use trying to surmise what had been
the original offence (non-payment of tithes, or
some moral evil) of which these three Luccombe
parishioners had been guilty.   The offence would
have been stated in the original sentence.   This
excommunication is a further declaration ; for the
excommunication was obliged, by English canon
law, to be repeated at the end of six months, and
to continue to be repeated at that interval
of time, provided the person or persons had not
meanwhile purged themselves by submission and
penance, and obtained the benefit of absolution.
The reason for the mention of the forty days, was
because of the law and custom of England,—
which in this respect differed from all other parts
of Christendom—the civil authority in the person
of the sheriff was bound to step in and imprison
excommunicated folk, until they made their
submission, provided that their wish *de excom-
municato capiendo* was sought for by the
diocesan or bishop.   On the same Sunday on
which these three Luccombe offenders were
denounced in their parish church, and all Christian

folk commanded to boycott them, the same excommunication was read during the service at the
cathedral church of Wells, and on the following
day the names and offences of those excommunicated were forwarded to the Archbishop of
the province.

On November 16th, 1628, the Archdeacon
issued another sentence of excommunication for
long-standing contempt against three Luccombe
parishioners, in very similar terms to the one
just quoted. The offenders were Moses Pugslie,
Amy Hawten, and Silvanus Band, and we may
conclude that Walter Pugslie and John Anton
had been meanwhile reconciled. This second
excommunication is somewhat damaged in
parts.

Another official document in the chest, which
has had a large marginal wafer seal attached,
was a marriage licence, issued by William.
Bishop of Bath and Wells, on March 12th,
1627. The contracting parties were John
Bryant, tailor, and Jane Jurdan, spinster. The
body of the document was in Latin, but at the end
is added in English: "If you knowe anie lawfull impediment to the contrary wherefore the
said parties ought not to be lawfully joyned to-

gether in matrimony you are not to procede to the solemnization thereof these presents notwith-standinge."

Another interesting, though damaged paper, for it was wrapped round some old pieces of tallow candle ends, proved to be a series of instructions put forth by the combined powers of church and state with regard to the regulations of authorised worship. The document is written throughout in a neat running hand. The provisions relative to lecturers would only apply to market towns, and those more populous places where such lecture-ships had been established. These lecturers were, as a rule, chosen by the parishioners, and paid by them after a voluntary fashion, or from some endowment left for that purpose. They were often the Sunday afternoon preachers, and usually preached on a week-day in addition. They were of Puritan origin, and intended in their foundation to specially exalt preaching, and to counteract the stiff, state preaching of the incumbent. Hence, the necessity of the church regulating their institution and methods, as is done by canons 36 and 37. This document is not dated, but it was obviously issued soon after the Restoration. There was legislation on the subject of lecturers and lectureships by 13 and 14 Charles II. c. 4, and 15 Charles II. c. 6.

"Instruction from his excellent Majestie to our Reverend Diocesan and by his Lordshippe given in charge to the clergie and all others whom it doth or shall concern within his Lordshippe's Diocese.

That ye declaration for yᵉ settling of all questions and differences Bee strictly observed of all parties.

That in all parishes the afternoon sermon may be turned into catechising by questions and answers when and wherever there is not some great cause apparent to break this ancient and profitable order.

That every lecturer doe read Divine service according to the Liturgie printed by Authority in their surplice and hood before the lecture.

That when a lecture is sett up in a Markett town it may be read by a companie of grave and orthodox Divines neare adjoining and of the same diocese and that they preach in gownes and not in Cassocks as too many use.

That if a Corporation do maintain a single lecturer he be not suffered to preach till he do profess his willingness to accept a benefice with care of soules in the same Incorporation and that he actually take such a benefice, or cure, soe soone as it shall be fairly procured for him.

That none under Noblemen and men qualified by lawe have any private chaplaine within their house.

That Divine service be deligently frequented as well for prayer and catechisms as sermons that can be had of it and that a particular note be taken of all such as absent themselves as Recusants or otherwise."

A curious example of seventeenth century

arithmetical problems came to light on the inner side of the lining paper of the loose cover of a parish account book, which began in the year 1702. It contained the statement of three sums or problems, with the space below each occupied by the working out of the figures by the scholar. They seem to us worth printing as a sample of the work done by our schoolboys about 1650 :—

"(1) Suppose a piece of Timber be 2 foot by 2 inches broad and 1 foot by 8 inches deep w^t is the true square of that piece say you.

(2) There be two Townes A and B lye south and north and betweene them 25 miles a third Towne as C lyes straight west from B 60 miles I demand the just distance A and C.

(3) A Towne wall being besieged which is 36 foot high and is moated round with a ditch 18 foot broad now the General commandeth Ladders to be made of that Length which may reach from ye edge of the ditch to the topp of the wall how many foot must the Ladder be in Length."

Three pages of parish accounts, very neatly kept, for the years 1633-5, were found. They thus begin :—

"Luccomb. Heare followeth the account of William Stock and Richard Blackmore, Churchwardens, John Balle and John Eame, Overseers for the Relleefe of the poore of the saith parish for this present yeere, Ano. dom. 1633."

Received by vertu of one Rate - viij$^{li.}$ xv$^{s.}$ iij^d

" Monthly distribucians beginning—

May 12. Imprimis payd unto the old overseers

ij^{li.} xiij^{s.} iiij^{d.}

Payd for a warrant of o^r ofice - vj^{d.}

To Jane Way - - - - ij^{s.}

To Florence Keene - - - viij^{d.}

To Alice Adam - - - - xvj^{d.}

To Jane Yomens - - - - ij^{s.}

To Edward Steere - - - ij^{s.}

Som is iij^{li.} j^s x^{d.}

The poor entries are made most carefully and totalled for each month, those relieved average six per month, and the same names are for the most part repeated. The relief varies from 8d. per month to 4s. From July onwards, the parish paid Alice Adam's house rent, which was 2s. 6d. per month. In August, 1s. is paid "for a trusse for Adam's boy," and in September, 8s. is paid to George Gore, "for healing ye widow Adams boy." In November, 5s. 8d. is paid "for a shroud for Robert Steere, and other charges at ye funerall." The poor were never then buried in coffins.

At the end of the year's accounts occur the following entries :—

"The viij^{li.} given by Laurance Byam, clarke, for the binding out of apprintices remaineth iij^{li.} in the hand of Anne Weber with Simon Pugsly, and is to be payd unto the overseers the xxvj^th day of July, Ano. dom. 1635. The other v^li. remaineth in our hands to be payd unto the new overseers."

In another hand.

"Somerset. Apud Dunster in com. pdt. xxi die April Ano. dni. 1634. If the overseers of the poore now nominated doe nott mak uppe this ten pounds full and all againe to bee put out with apprentices accordinge to the good and memorable intention of Mr. Lawrence Byam, deceased, they shall pay the fortie shillinges which now comes short themselves ; and wee doe order that the goods of one Richard Daniel, the late servant of John Ball, which hee left in his said masters custodie when hee ranne away for basterdie upon the accusation of Agnes Duddridge, bee sould for the best profitt and advantage towards the releafe of the bastard.

Tho. Windham.

Tho. Luterell."

The above are interesting instances of the way in which the justices, according to the poor law legislation of 39 and 43 Elizabeth, intervened in the regulating of parish officers' accounts. The justices above-named, Windham or Wyndham, and Luttrell, were of the well-known west country families resident respectively at the adjacent little towns of Minehead and Dunster. Just one example was preserved in the Luccombe chest of the old form of appointing two parish overseers, who, together with the churchwardens, were to

18

raise competent sums for the necessary relief of the aged and indigent, and to provide work for such as were able but could not get employment. This document, two years later than the poor's account cited above, is signed by the same magistrates.

> "Somerset. Wee whose names bee subscribed Justices of the peace within the said countye of Somerset and neere unto the parish of Luccombe in the said countye have accordinge to the statute in that case made and provided and appointed Robert Phillips and Amos Byckham together with the Churchwardens of the said parish to bee Overseers of the Poore there for this yeare next ensuinge. Witness our hands and seales the xxij day of April, Ano R. R. Caroli Anglie etc 1635.
>
> Tho : Wyndham   (Seal)
> Tho : Luttrell   (Seal)

It is well known to ecclesiologists that up to comparatively recent times, a variety of notices, that would now considerably startle demure congregations, were given out in parish churches. Not a few Acts of Parliament, even of the beginning of the present century, provide for declarations and announcements being made, by such officials as parish constables, on the Sunday in church at the conclusion of service. But so far as our acquaintance with old parochial documents extends, the Luccombe chest is the only one that has yielded absolute evidence of announcements being made in church in the seventeenth century about strayed cattle. By no means the least interesting of the curious medley of fragments so strangely preserved in this West Somerset village was one of which the following is a copy :—

> "The Clerke shal give nottice on Trinitie Sondaye after divine service is ended publickly in the Chuche that one score and three straye sheepe hav bin vounde in David Pugsley his bartone with a clippette in ye lefte eare. Alsoe that a redde cowe hath bene pinned by the pyndere of East Luckham."

The writing is good, too good probably for the village constable, and is most likely that of the rector or curate. The sheep had doubtless strayed off the closely adjacent Exmoor. The " Zomerzet," v for f may be noticed in " vounde " for " found." This paper is not dated, but there can be no doubt that it is of the reign of Charles the First.

Index.

LIST OF PUBLICATIONS

OF

WILLIAM ANDREWS & CO.,

THE HULL PRESS.

" Valuable and interesting."—*The Times.*

" Readable as well as instructive."—*The Globe.*

" A valuable addition to any library."—*Derbyshire Times.*

The Bygone Series.

In this series the following volumes are included, and issued at 7s. 6d. each. Demy 8vo., cloth gilt.

These books have been favourably reviewed in the leading critical journals of England and America.

Carefully written articles by recognised authorities are included on history, castles, abbeys, biography, romantic episodes, legendary lore, traditional stories, curious customs, folk-lore, etc., etc.

The works are illustrated by eminent artists, and by the reproduction of quaint pictures of the olden time.

HULL : WILLIAM ANDREWS & CO., THE HULL PRESS.

London : Simpkin, Marshall, Hamilton, Kent, & Co., Ltd.

SECOND EDITION   Bound in cloth gilt, demy 8vo., 6s.

Curiosities of the Church:

Studies of Curious Customs, Services, and Records,

By WILLIAM ANDREWS, F.R.H.S.,

AUTHOR OF "HISTORIC ROMANCE," "FAMOUS FROSTS AND
FROST FAIRS," "HISTORIC YORKSHIRE," ETC.

CONTENTS:

Early Religious Plays: being the Story of the English Stage in
its Church Cradle Days—The Caistor Gad-Whip Manorial
Service—Strange Serpent Stories—Church Ales—Rush-Bearing
—Fish in Lent—Concerning Doles—Church Scrambling Chari-
ties—Briefs—Bells and Beacons for Travellers by Night—Hour
Glasses in Churches—Chained Books in Churches—Funeral
Effigies—Torchlight Burials—Simple Memorials of the Early
Dead—The Romance of Parish Registers—Dog Whippers and
Sluggard Wakers—Odd Items from Old Accounts—A carefully
compiled Index.

—◉ ILLUSTRATED. ◉—

Press Opinions.

A volume both entertaining and instructive, throwing much light on the manners
and customs of bygone generations of Churchmen, and will be read to-day with much
interest.—*Newbery House Magazine.*
An extremely interesting volume.—*North British Daily Mail.*
A work of lasting interest.—*Hull Examiner.*
The reader will find much in this book to interest, instruct, and amuse.— *Home
Chimes.*
We feel sure that many will feel grateful to Mr. Andrews for having produced such
an interesting book.—*The Antiquary.*
A volume of great research and striking interest.--*The Book-buyer (New York.)*
A valuable book.—*Literary World (Boston, U.S.A.).*
An admirable book.—*Sheffield Independent.*
An interesting, handsomely got up volume. . . . Mr. Andrews is always chatty
and expert in making a paper on a dry subject exceedingly readable.—*Newcastle Courant.*
Mr. William Andrews' new book, 'Curiosities of the Church,' adds another to the
series by which he has done so much to popularise antiquarian studies. . . The book,
it should be added, has some quaint illustrations, and its rich matter is made available
for reference by a full and carefully compiled index.—*Scotsman.*

HULL : WILLIAM ANDREWS & CO., THE HULL PRESS.
London : Simpkin, Marshall, Hamilton, Kent, & Co., Ltd.

Elegantly bound in cloth gilt, demy 8vo., 6s.

Old Church Lore.

By WILLIAM ANDREWS, F.R.H.S.,

Author of " Curiosities of the Church," " Old-Time Punishments,"
" Historic Romance," etc.

CONTENTS.

The Right of Sanctuary—The Romance of Trial—A Fight between the Mayor of Hull and the Archbishop of York—Chapels on Bridges—Charter Horns—The Old English Sunday—The Easter Sepulchre—St. Paul's Cross—Cheapside Cross—The Biddenden Maids Charity —Plagues and Pestilences—A King curing an Abbot of Indigestion—The Services and Customs of Royal Oak Day—Marrying in a White Sheet—Marrying under the Gallows—Kissing the Bride—Hot Ale at Weddings —Marrying Children—The Passing Bell—Concerning Coffins—The Curfew Bell—Curious Symbols of the Saints —Acrobats on Steeples—A carefully-prepared Index.

ILLUSTRATED.

PRESS OPINIONS

" A worthy work on a deeply interesting subject. . . . We commend this book strongly."—*European Mail.*

" An interesting volume."—*The Scotsman.*

" Contains much that will interest and instruct."—*Glasgow Herald.*

" The author has produced a book which is at once entertaining and valuable, and which is also entitled to unstinted praise on the ground of its admirable printing and binding."—*Shields Daily Gazette.*

" Mr. Andrews' book does not contain a dull page. . . . Deserves to meet with a very warm welcome."—*Yorkshire Post.*

" Mr. Andrews, in 'Old Church Lore,' makes the musty parchments and records he has consulted redolent with life and actuality, and has added to his works a most interesting volume, which, written in a light and easy narrative style, is anything but of the 'dry-as-dust' order. The book is handsomely got up, being both bound and printed in an artistic fashion."—*Northern Daily News.*

HULL: WILLIAM ANDREWS & CO., THE HULL PRESS.
London: Simpkin, Marshall, Hamilton, Kent, & Co., Ltd.

Elegantly bound in cloth gilt, demy 8vo., 7s. 6d.

THE DOCTOR,
IN HISTORY, LITERATURE, FOLK-LORE, ETC.,
Edited by WILLIAM ANDREWS, F.R.H.S.

CONTENTS:

—◉ ILLUSTRATED. ◉—

"A rich fund of quaint and out-of-the-way information relating to physicians and the healing art will be found in the 'The Doctor' . . . got up in neat and attractive form."—*Leeds Mercury.*

"Most interesting. . . . An immense amount of information that will be new to most readers."—*The News,* edited by Rev. Charles Bullock, B.D.

"'The Doctor' is an attractive miscellany of the type so pleasantly associated with Mr. William Andrews' name, in which he has, as he tells us, 'attempted to bring together from the pens of several authors, who have written expressly for this book, the more interesting phases of the history, literature, folk-lore, etc., of the medical profession.' The subject is an interesting one. and is treated by Mr. Andrews and his several contributors in a genial, gossiping, and not too abstruse fashion."—*The Times.*

"The volume, besides being readable and entertaining to all who are interested in bygone fashions and characters of the medical profession, is of some value as a work of reference on its antiquities . . . An admirable index."—*Scotsman.*

"An excellent volume. . . . The book is elegantly got up."— *Chester Courant.*

HULL: WILLIAM ANDREWS & CO., THE HULL PRESS.
London: Simpkin, Marshall, Hamilton, Kent, & Co., Ltd.

Elegantly Bound, Crown 8vo., price 2s. 6d.

Faces · oŋ · the · Queen's · Highway,

By FLO. JACKSON.

THOUGH oftenest to be found in a pensive mood, the writer of this very dainty volume of sketches is always very sweet and winning. She has evidently a true artist's love of nature, and in a few lines can limn an autumn landscape full of colour, and the life which is on the down slope. And she can tell a very taking story, as witness the sketch "At the Inn," and "The Master of White Hags," and all her characters are real, live flesh-and-blood people, who do things naturally, and give very great pleasure to the reader accordingly. Miss Jackson's gifts are of a very high order.—*Aberdeen Free Press.*

A charmingly written series of sketches and stories by Flo Jackson, published under the happy title "Faces on the Queen's Highway." The writer possesses descriptive powers of a high order, and her "visionary glimpses of the passers on the patch of highway beyond the curtained window," appeals strongly to one's better and nobler feelings.—*Chester Courant.*

This volume bears the name, as its author, of Flo Jackson, a talented writer, whose sketches and stories we have often read with pleasure. We can promise the same experience for readers of this volume, which contains some of Miss Jackson's typical work in prose. "In Winter Mood," "At the Inn," "The Journey of the Leaves," "Safe at Last," and the sketches in "Faces" are specimens of a high standard of literary excellence. With a poetic and imaginative nature the writer combines a happy power of expression, and she is thus enabled to paint a picture which easily arrests the attention. "At the Inn," already named, is a short story, which for its artistic effect and its pathos would sustain the reputation of one of our leading authors. Throughout the book there is a spirit of tender refinement; while there are numerous features likely to attract the reader, there are none to repel him. The prevailing style is as unconventional as the "introduction," which is a pretty departure from the orthodox mode of bowing to the reader.—*Bristol Observer.*

HULL: WILLIAM ANDREWS & CO., THE HULL PRESS.
London: Simpkin, Marshall, Hamilton, Kent, & Co., Ld.

legantly bound in cloth gilt, Demy 8vo., Price 6s.

Bygone England:
Social Studies in Its Historic Byways and Highways.
By WILLIAM ANDREWS, F.R.H.S.

CONTENTS :—Under Watch and Ward—Under Lock and Key—The Practice of Pledging—The minstrel in the Olden Time—Curious Landholding Customs—Curiosities of Slavery in England—Buying and Selling in the Olden Time –Curious Fair Customs—Old Pre· judices against Coal—The Sedan Chair—Running Footmen—The Early Days of the Umbrella—A Talk about Tea—Concerning Coffee— The Horn Book—Fighting Cocks in Schools—Bull Baiting—The Badge of Poverty—Patents to wear Nightcaps—A Foolish Fashion— Wedding Notices in the Last Century—Selling Wives—The Story of the Tinder Box—The Invention of Friction matches—Body Snatching —Christmas under the Commonwealth—Under the mistletoe Bough— A carefully prepared Index.

" We welcome ' Bygone England.' It is another of Mr. Andrews' meritorious achievements in the path of popularising archæological and old time information without in any way writing down to an ignoble level."—*The Antiquary.*

" A delightful volume for all who love to dive into the origin of social habits and customs, and to penetrate into the byways of history."—*Liverpool Daily Post.*

" There is a large mass of information in this capital volume, and it is so pleasantly put that many will be tempted to study it. Mr. Andrews has done his work with great skill."—*London Quarterly Review.*

Bound in cloth gilt, demy 8vo., price 7s. 6d. Only 500 copies printed, and each copy numbered.

The Monumental Brasses of Lancashire and Cheshire.
With some Account of the Persons Represented.
Illustrated with Engravings from Drawings by the Author.
By JAMES L. THORNELY.

" Mr. Thornely's book will be eagerly sought by all lovers of monumental brasses."—*London Quarterly Review.*

" Local archæologists will give a hearty welcome to this book."— *Manchester Guardian.*

" Mr. Thornely has produced a very interesting volume, as he has not only figured every monumental brass within the two counties to which he has confined his researches, but in every case he has given a description also, and in some instances the genealogical information is of a high order of value."—*The Tablet.*

" The book is wonderfully readable for its kind, and is evidently the result of careful and painstaking labour. The chapters are well condensed, nowhere burdened with verbiage, yet sufficiently full to serve the purpose in view. The illustrations of the various brasses are exceedingly well done, and add much value and interest to the work, which should become popular in Lancashire and Cheshire."— *Warrington Guardian.*

HULL: WILLIAM ANDREWS & CO., THE HULL PRESS.
London : Simpkin, Marshall, Hamilton, Kent, & Co., Ltd.

Just published. Crown 8vo., 330 pp. A Portrait of the Author, and other Illustrations. Price 3/6.

𝕮𝖍𝖊 (𝕽𝖊𝖉, (𝕽𝖊𝖉 𝖂𝖎𝖓𝖊,

BY THE REV. J. JACKSON WRAY.

"This, as its name implies, is a temperance story, and is told in the lamented author's most graphic style. We have never read anything so powerful since 'Danesbury House,' and this book in stern and pathetic earnestness even excels that widely-known book. It is worthy a place in every Sunday School and village library ; and, as the latest utterance of one whose writings are so deservedly popular, it is sure of a welcome. It should give decision to some whose views about Local Option are hazy."—*Joyful News.*

"The story is one of remarkable power."—*The Temperance Record.*

"An excellent and interesting story."—*The Temperance Chronicle.*

"It is written in a graphic and conversational style, abounding with rapidly-succeeding incidents, which arrest and sustain the interest of the reader."—*The League Journal.*

"It is just the right sort of book for a prize or present, and should find a place in every Band of Hope and Sunday School library."—*The Abstainer's Advocate.*

"A pathetic interest attaches to this volume, it being the last legacy of Mr. Jackson Wray. It is a story with a purpose—to advocate the claims of total abstinence. The plot is laid in a small village of the East Riding of Yorkshire, and the author sketches the awful ravages of intemperance in that small community. The victims include a minister, doctor, and many others who found, when too late, that the red, red wine biteth like a serpent. Though terribly realistic, the picture is drawn from life, and every tragical incident had its counterpart among the dwellers in that village. It is a healthy and powerful temperance tale, and a fearless exposure of the quiet drinking that was so common in respectable circles thirty years ago. It should find a place in our school libraries, to be read by elder scholars."—*Methodist Times.*

"This is a powerful story, the last from the pen of an indefatigable worker and true friend of the total abstinence cause. The scene of the o'er true tale is laid in East Yorkshire, the author's native district, which he knew and loved so well. The characters appear to be drawn from life, and every chapter has a vivid and terrible interest. The friendship between old Aaron Brigham and Little Kitty is touching. The tale of trouble, sorrow, and utter ruin wrought by the demon of strong drink might well rouse every man, woman, and child to fight the destroyer, which, in the unfolding of the story, we see enslaving minister and people, shaming the Christian Church, breaking hearts all round, and wrecking the dearest hopes of individuals and families. A striking and pitiful tale, not overdrawn.—*Alliance News.*

Hull : William Andrews & Co., The Hull Press.
London : Simpkin, Marshall, Hamilton, Kent & Co., Ltd.
And all Booksellers.

www.ingramcontent.com/pod-product-compliance
Lightning Source LLC
Chambersburg PA
CBHW020853020726
47497CB00005B/1390